CAUSATION AND FUNCTIONALISM
IN SOCIOLOGY

CAUSATION
AND
FUNCTIONALISM
IN SOCIOLOGY

by
WSEVOLOD W. ISAJIW

SCHOCKEN BOOKS · NEW YORK

Published in U.S.A. 1968
by Schocken Books Inc.
67 Park Avenue
New York, N.Y. 10016

© *Wsevolod W. Isajiw 1968*

Library of Congress Catalog Card Number 68-16657

Contents

Preface

What follows is an analysis of functionalism by means of the notion of causality. It is a study of functionalism, yet also an explication of the notion of causality through its application to a sociological theory.

Construction of sociological theory, besides its empirical groundwork, requires resolution of many metasociological issues. For all the pedantry of empirical research, development of sociological theory has been inhibited by the fear or reluctance of sociological thinkers to take on issues which go beyond the "acceptable" methodological values. One such issue is the problem of causal explanation. Perhaps, in developing any general theory, such as functionalism or symbolic interactionism, progress can be made when the theory's causal implications are assessed. Indeed, functionalism and symbolic interactionism are two salient theoretical approaches in sociology today. Functionalism, however, stands out as an approach peculiarly sociological.

It is difficult for me to find the root of my interest in functionalism, but, I am sure, part of it is the challenge offered by the works of Talcott Parsons.

I wish to express gratitude to all those who have contributed to the realization of this study. In particular, appreciation is due to Dr. R. Cletus Brady for supervision and crisp criticism of this work, when it was written as a dissertation, to Dr. C. Joseph Nuesse, Rev. Allan B. Wolter, O.F.M., and Rev. Raymond H. Potvin.

Special thanks go to my wife, Christine, for her stimulating encouragement, to my parents, for their quiet but constant interest, to Francisco E. Borja, for his helpful philosophical discussions, and to all my friends and associates whose constant reminders have contributed in their own manner to the materialization of this work. Lastly, special thanks are due to my brother, George, who by his valuable editorial suggestions turned out to be much more than a typist.

Windsor, Ontario   W. W. ISAJIW
October 1967

vii

Chapter I

INTRODUCTION

There is agreement among philosophers of science that scientific explanation of phenomena consists in deducing propositions from other more general propositions. Explanation is essentially deduction. Phenomena can be explained if any proposition about the relationships between the phenomena can be deduced from some more general propositions. These general propositions are known as laws. Indeed the objective of science is establishment of systems of general laws, but the whole value of general laws is that specific empirical phenomena can be explained in their terms. Explanation is attained when observations about empirical phenomena can be logically deduced from these laws.[1] Thus the explanans contains a major and a minor premise, whereas the explanandum becomes a conclusion of the syllogism. The major premise is a general law or a set of such laws. The minor premise is a statement about an empirical situation which is associated with the phenomenon to be explained but at the same time it states that the specific situation is an instance in which the law can be operative. The conclusion is a statement which affirms that because the phenomenon to be explained is associated with the situation in which the law can be operative, it actually is an instance in which the law is operative.

For example, if the explanandum is the inefficiency or dissatisfaction of cooks in a restaurant, the explanatory syllogism will be as follows:

Major: Ordering of males by females renders males inefficient.
Minor: Waitresses order cooks.

> *Instantial inference:* Waitresses are females, cooks are males; hence, this is an instance of females ordering males.

Conclusion: Cooks are inefficient.

Major: Persons in lower status ordering persons in higher status make persons in higher status dissatisfied.
Minor: Waitresses order cooks.

> *Instantial inference:* Waitresses are in a lower status than cooks; hence, this is an instance of persons in lower status ordering persons in higher status.

Conclusion: Cooks are dissatisfied.

Deduction, however, can proceed from different levels of generality and from different types of assumptions. Hence, there can be various types of explanation. A major distinction is between explanation provided by statistical research and that provided by theory. In the first case, the generality of propositions from which deductions are made is low, essentially that of empirical quantitative level. It is explanation of statistical observations in terms of purely probabilistic generalizations[2]

Explanation through probabilistic generalization is perhaps the most common type in sociological literature. The deductive aspect of this form of explanation is involved in the procedures which establish relations of dependence between quantified phenomena. They are procedures of controlled correlation of variables with the aim of discovering the best correlation.

Ernest Nagel mentions a typical example of a two-by-two table. Thus if in a sample of 205 women working in factories, 100 of whom are married and the rest single, 25 of the former are absentees, but only 10 of the latter, then the implicit statistical observations are that (1) 'in the population of women factory employees, the relative frequency of absentees among those married is 25/100 or .25' and (2) 'in the population of women factory employees, the relative fre-

quency of absentees among those single is 10/105, or .09+'.
Each of these observations can be subsumed under a general proposition stating that 'In the population K, the relative frequency with which the attribute x occurs in the class of those having the attribute y is $f_{x,y}$.' If this is so, then the following deduction can be made: 'Since the first of these relative frequencies is significantly greater than the second, there appears to be a definite connection between the marital status of women and absenteeism.'[3]

This offers an explanation of the above stated statistical observations. But it is a weak, unconvincing, unsatisfying explanation. Only a fraction of married women are absentees. One wants to be more certain than that about the relations of the statistical numbers. Hence, the next step in this type of explanation is factorial analysis in order to find out if there is any greater dependence between the statistical variables. An assumption can be made that the observed association between the marital state and absenteeism can be accounted for by a third factor, say household work, when the population of the women workers is stratified into those who do significant household work and those who do not. The previous association is assumed to be spurious and the generalization in terms of which the explanation proceeds now states that: 'If population K is divided into two classes, T (those who possess the third characteristic) and T (those who do not possess the third characteristic), then there is no significant statistical relation between x and y in either class of K.'[4]

The minor premise of this deduction shows that in both classes of K the frequency of x in the y group is not significantly different from the frequency of x in the y group. Thus, as Nagel explains, suppose that among the working women it is found that 76 do a great deal of housework and 129 do not, and that in the former group of those who are married (y), 24 are absentees (x) and 33 are not (x), while of those who are single (y), 8 are absentees but 11 are not; in the latter group of those who are married, 1 is an absentee and 42 are not, while of those who are single 2 are absentees and 84 are not. In the housework group, the frequency of x in y is 24/57 or .42 and is equal to the frequency of x in y, group, i.e. 8/19 or .42. The same holds true of the non-housework group. Since these frequencies are equal, this then is a case which can be subsumed under the original generalization and we can conclude that there is no significant correlation between x and y.

Further logical steps in this type of explanation would be to show that there is a significant correlation between x and T, and y and T, or else to show that there is a correlation between x and T but not y and T, or between y and T but not between x and T. The ultimate ideal in such factorial analysis is to arrive either at a perfect correlation according to which a total dependence of one variable upon another could be claimed, or else a total independence of one variable from another.[5] But even before the correlation of specific variables is obtained, the aim of explanatory analysis is to find what we shall term the *focus of determinacy*. Two ideas are involved in this phrase, that of focus and that of determinacy. The *focus* of determinacy refers to the area in which a proper explanans of some explanandum can be found. It refers to the problem of finding the explanans: it does not refer to any single independent variable but to a universe of discourse in which such a variable or set of such variables or generalizations referring to such variables can be found. In the above example, the problem of the focus of determinacy is that of finding the explanans for x in the category of variables represented by y (apparently directly related variables), or in the T category ('third factor' variables), or neither in the y type category or T category. Translated into the suggested qualitative statements, the problem of the focus of determinacy is that of finding the explanans for absenteeism either in the area of marital status or in activity like household work or in neither of these areas.

Explanation on the statistical level, however, though

essential for science, is nevertheless too limited. The general propositions from which deductions are made are in effect *ad hoc* hypotheses. As such they are limited to the specific sample data collected at the specific time. Furthermore, this type of explanation does not make any assumptions as to the subject matter studied—the same type of factorial analysis can be employed to study subjects other than human behaviour. The general propositions are simply about quantitative frequency distributions.

It is on the level of systematic theory that the *ad hoc* situation can be transcended and the general propositions from which other propositions, including the qualitative hypotheses through which the *ad hoc* hypotheses can be explained, can be deduced without total limitation to a sample or time element. Also on this level non-quantitative assumptions as to the subject matter have to be made.[6] Systematic theory is a set of interdependent propositions which permit deduction of a variety of other propositions and a variety of hypotheses. As George Homans says:

> A theory of a phenomenon consists of a series of propositions, each stating a relationship between properties of nature. But not every kind of sentence qualifies as such a proposition. The propositions do not consist of definitions of the properties: the construction of a conceptual scheme is an indispensable part of theoretical work but it is not itself theory. Nor may a proposition simply say that there is some relationship between the properties. Instead, if there is some change in one of the properties, it must, at least begin to specify what the change in the other property will be. If one of the properties is absent, the other will also be absent; or if one of the properties increases in value, the other will too. The properties, the variables, may be probabilities.[7]

One basic earmark of a good scientific theory is consistency of its propositions and sets of propositions. Contradictions between propositions often result from the fact that they are derived from different assumptions, in particular different assumptions about the focus of determinacy. This, in effect means that such propositions are parts of two different theories rather than one.[8] More detailed aspects of systematic theories, as well as the use of models, will be discussed later in this study. At the moment it is necessary to distinguish between the types of systematic explanation advanced in sociology.

Nagel points out that in the social science literature two types of theoretical explanation have been outstanding, that of methodological individualism and that of functionalism. From the point of view of explanation, the basic difference between the two approaches is their divergence as to the focus of determinacy. Methodological individualism attempts to place the focus of determinacy in the psychological realm, so that all explanation of social phenomena could be reduced to psychological terms, i.e., attributes of individuals.[9] Social behaviouristic theories, including symbolic interactionism, can be classified in this category.[10] The functional explanation, on the other hand, places the focus of determinacy in the attributes of collectivities. These positions thus derive from different philosophical assumptions.

Functionalism, however, presents a special problem of explanation because if the focus of determinacy is placed in the attributes of collectivities rather than individuals, one implicit assumption is that systems of relations between individual human beings, in their own right, are capable of exercising a determining influence upon their behaviour. This type of holism is akin to vitalistic explanation in biology.[11]

The precise nature of the explanation provided by functionalism has been a much debated issue. In the more recent discussion three positions critical of functionalism have been rather prominent. All of them will be discussed more fully later on in the study. Here they are simply identified. First, one position holds that functionalism is a valid method of explanation, but not a distinct method since all science, by studying the relation of parts to the whole, follows the same procedure as functionalism. Hence functionalism as a unique form of explanation is viewed as only a myth which will be dispelled with time. This is the position of Kingsley Davis.[12]

The second position, best stated by Carl Hempel, argues that functionalism, though a distinct method of explanation, is nevertheless a rather weak and inadequate method, producing a rather dubious type of explanation.[13]

The third position, as emphatically stated by George Homans holds, that although functionalism is a method of research, it is not a method of explanation. It is not a substantive scientific theory because it has failed to fulfil requirements of a scientific theory—it has not produced a system of propositions which can specify what change in properties of a phenomenon will take place if there is change in other properties of the phenomenon.[14] This position actually argues for methodological individualism on the ground that the human actions which make up the collectivity or any of its aspects are in fact the same actions that make up the individual personality. Hence, if we try to explain real behaviour we must explain it in terms that refer to real phenomena rather than hypostatical phenomena. The latter are explainable only in terms of the former.

As stated above, a central problem of explanation is the problem of the focus of determinacy. According to Davis' critique of functionalism, the focus of determinacy in functionalism is not different from that of any other scientific explanation. According to Hempel's criticism, the focus of determinacy in functionalism fails to produce propositions giving satisfying explanations; hence it is a rather weak focus. According to Homans' critique, functionalist focus of determinacy is in effect no different from that of methodological individualism.

This brings up the problem of the meaning of determinacy. As understood in this study, determinacy refers to the relation of dependence between phenomena. If a phenomenon in any way depends upon another phenomenon or set of phenomena, we can say that it is in some way determined by it. All explanation aims at discovering the precise nature of this dependence in any specific case. Hence, one means by which to evaluate a scientific theory is through the study of the determinacy involved in its propositions. Several types of determinacy have been distinguished by the philosophers of science. Among these types, however, causal determinacy has been given the most prominent discussion.[15]

As an attempt to understand more fully the type of explanation provided by functionalism, this study will examine the causal implications of the functional theory in sociology. In contemporary sociology, functionalism presents the most important single attempt to construct a scientific system of explanation that is peculiarly sociological. The aim of this study is to evaluate functionalism from the point of view of its causal import.

Extremely little has been written on this subject. There is no single sizeable work dealing with the question, and most of the material on the subject is rather cursory.[16] The present study, therefore, can be considered as a pioneer work in this area. Underlying it is the assumption that causal explanation is ultimately the type of explanation which is most intellectually satisfying, and that scientists look for such explanation in their research, either explicitly or implicitly. As MacIver states:

> It is . . . not unreasonable to conclude that all relations between things, if not themselves relations of causation, at least have somewhere a causal ground. Consider, for example, the difference between correlation and causal relation. Correlation . . . is not a relation between things at all. The relation between quantitative variables is a mathematical relation, a relation of index number that *may* lead us to discover a relation of things. Correlation as such has no dynamic significance, any more than have the resemblances between animals and clouds. We seek out correlations in our search for knowledge of the relations of things. . . . We look for correlations only when we suspect they may be causally significant.[17]

8

This study, therefore, concerns the metasociological aspects of functionalism. The focus is on assessing the causal explanatory value of functionalism. In particular, functionalism will be examined as found in the writings of Talcott Parsons, Robert K. Merton, and several of their commentators. In many ways the notions of functionalism of the two men will be contrasted. They present two different approaches to functional explanation, each deriving from a different set of assumptions. The Parsonian notion of functionalism will be seen to be more far-reaching in causal implications.

The notion of causality and its different types employed in this study is based on the works of Mario Bunge and P. Janet.[18] The latter work is old, and it might be objected that it has been uncritically applied in this study. Yet its statement of the problem of finality is clear, and if nothing else, it has heuristic value for the purposes of this study.

Because it combines two approaches, functional and causal, both of which have been surrounded by controversy at one time or another, the scope for this study is wide and therefore, necessarily, the study will not solve all the relevant problems or answer all the pertinent questions. Yet it is hoped that it will throw enough light on what functional explanation in sociology is to stimulate further development of its logic and to make possible its more fruitful application to empirical research.

The remainder of this chapter will consider the aims and the definition of functionalism, an explanation of the notion of causality as accepted in this study, and a brief statement of the causal problem in functionalism. Chapter II will discuss how what is here called *productive causality* is implicated in functionalism, and Chapters III and IV will consider what is called the *telecausal* implications of functionalism. The final Chapter will try to evaluate the explanatory value of functionalism in view of its causal implications and in view of the objections expressed by some contemporary critics.

AIM, PROCEDURE AND DEFINITION
OF FUNCTIONALISM

Functionalism in sociology appears as a recent attempt to integrate sociological knowledge into a form of theory. The question which functionalism tries to answer is how social phenomena can be treated as dynamically inter-dependent variables. The emphasis is on what Parsons calls the 'dynamic interest of theory', resulting in 'dynamic knowledge'.[19] It is only in reference to this dynamic interest that functionalism can be properly understood. Dynamic knowledge is an ideal toward which functionalism strives. It is held to be an ideal of all scientific enquiry. Both Parsons and Merton are in agreement on this. In its ideal form, dynamic analysis is analogous to mathematical analysis. Parsons explains this meaning of dynamic analysis as follows:

> The essential feature of dynamic analysis in the fullest sense is the treatment of a body of *interdependent* phenomena simul-taneously, in the mathematical sense. The simplest case is the analysis of the effect of variation in one antecedent factor, but this ignores the reciprocal effect of these changes on this factor. The ideal solution is the possession of a logically complete system of dynamic generalizations which can state all the elements of reciprocal interdependence between all the variables of the system. The ideal has, in the formal sense, been attained only in the systems of differential equations of analytical mechanics. All other sciences are limited to a more 'primitive' level of symbolic theoretical analysis. [20]

Merton expresses this ideal when he states that 'the word function has its most precise significance in mathematics, where it refers to a variable considered in relation to one or more other variables in terms of which it may be expressed or on the value of which its own value depends'.[21]

The essential problem of dynamic analysis is, as Parsons points out, the possibility of treating a body, i.e., a system, of variables simultaneously. This means the possibility of shifting deductively from one aspect or part of a system of variables to another, so that 'it is possible to say that if the facts in A sector are *W* and *X*, those in B sector must be *Y* and *Z*'.[22] Parsons is much more concerned with the problem of dynamic analysis than Merton. He discusses it at length and penetrates its ramifications. As we shall see later, Merton's concern is primarily elsewhere. Perhaps as a consequence, he leaves some important problems of functional analysis unanswered.

Nevertheless, both Parsons and Merton recognize that at least in the present state of sociology the ideal of dynamic analysis is unrealizable. Merton points out that, as practised in sociology and social anthropology, this ideal has been expressed in a more extended and imprecise form by such notions as 'functional interdependence', 'functional relations', 'mutually dependent variations', etc.[23] Parsons tries to explain why dynamic analysis in its fullest sense cannot be realized today, and then goes on to propose his theory of structural-functional analysis as the best possible substitute for dynamic analysis under the circumstances.

Parsons: The Problem of Dynamic Analysis

A *system* of variables that can permit dynamic analysis, i.e., deductive shift from one set of variables to another, necessarily implies, according to Parsons, definite and uniform relations among the variables. This is the basic general meaning of the system—interdependence of variables. Interdependence involves both independence and dependence of variables. That is, 'all interdependent variables are, by virtue of the fact that they are variables in a system, interdependent with other variables'.[24] A dependent variable is 'one which stands in a *fixed* relation to another such that, if the value of *x* (an independent variable) is known, that of *y* (the dependent variable) can be deduced from it with the aid of the formula stating their relation and without the aid of any other empirical data. This means that the value and explanation of any one variable is its relation to relations of other variables. That is, the value of *y* (dependent variable) depends not only on its relation to x (independent variable in reference to y), and z (another independent variable in reference to y), but also on the relation between x and z (dependent variables in reference to one another). It follows —and this is crucial if there is to be a full dynamic analysis— that the value of any one variable cannot be completely determined unless its relation to all other variables in a system is known, as well as relations of all other variables among themselves. All such relations in a system Parsons calls 'uniformities of dynamic process'.[25]

In regard to social phenomena, such analysis of the uniformities of dynamic process in today's sociology, says Parsons, is non-existent. That is so because 'we simply are not in a position to "catch" the uniformities of dynamic process in the social system except here and there'. Dynamic process in the study of social phenomena refers to the action process of its components. Unfortunately, our knowledge of this process as relevant to the social system is very fragmentary. Hence the problem: How, under such circumstances, is it possible to mobilize our knowledge of the action process and its components for the study of social phenomena, so as to attain as much as possible a dynamic analysis? Parsons' answer is his structural-functional theory. To cite Parsons:

> The most essential condition of successful dynamic analysis is continual and systematic reference of every problem to the state of the system as a whole. If it is not possible to provide for that by explicit inclusion of every relevent fact as the value of a variable which is included in the dynamic analysis at that point, there must be some method of simplification. Logically, this is possible only through the removal of some generalized categories from the role of variables and their treatment as constants. An analytical system of the type of mechanics does just this for certain elements *outside* the system which are conditional to it. But it is also logically feasible *within* the system. This is essentially what happens when structural categories are used in the treatment of dynamic problems.

Their function is to simplify the dynamic problems to the point where they are manageable without the possibility of refined mathematical analysis. At the same time the loss, which is very great, is partly compensated by relating all problems explicitly and systematically to the total system. For the structure of a system as described in the context of a generalized conceptual scheme is a genuinely technical analytical tool. It ensures that nothing of vital importance is inadvertently overlooked, and ties in loose ends, giving determinacy to problems and solutions. It minimizes the danger, so serious to common-sense thinking, of filling gaps by resort to uncriticized residual categories.[26]

The construction of Parsons' alternative to a full dynamic analysis, i.e., the structural-functional theory, consists of three steps. First, to simplify the problem of dealing with a complex of interrelated variables, groups of them are removed and treated as structural categories, i.e., not as variables, but as constants. A complete system of such categories is required so as to provide adequate description of the empirical social system. As a conceptual scheme, the system of structural categories becomes a setting for dynamic analysis. Structural categories become points of reference for organization of dynamic knowledge. They can do this because now they appear as constants, that is, defined independently, not in terms of other variables. As such, however, they are only a tool, and in proportion as dynamic knowledge advances, they lose their independent explanatory value and turn into variables again. Parsons insists that 'as dynamic knowledge is extended the *independent* explanatory significance of structural categories evaporates'.[27] For example, norms, values, roles are structural categories in terms of which different social phenomena can be explained. But to the extent that norms, values and roles themselves become explained in terms of other categories, they lose their independent explanatory significance and acquire the character of variables. Hence, the sole task of structural categories is to enable handling of the complex body of relations of variables. Thus Parsons writes:

It should be noted that in mechanics the structure of the system does not enter in as a distinct theoretical element. For descriptive purposes, it is of course relevant for any state of the system. But on the dynamic plane it dissolves into process and interdependence. This calls attention to the important fact that the structure and process are highly relative categories. Structure does not refer to any ontological stability in phenomena but only to a relative stability—to sufficiently stable uniformities in the results of underlying processes so that their constancy within certain limits is a workable pragmatic assumption.[28]

The second step in building the structural-functional theory is linking the structural categories to the dynamically variable elements in the system. This is done through the concept of 'function' whose role is 'to provide criteria of the importance of dynamic factors and processes within the system'. The dynamic variables, as dynamic processes, are linked with the structural categories by establishing how relevant they are to the total social system that is conceived in terms of structural categories. Establishment of relevance means determining the consequences of dynamic processes (action processes and their components) for the total system in terms of maintenance or change, i.e., determining whether these processes maintain the stability of the social system or produce in it a change, whether they integrate it or disrupt it.[29] Assessment of such relevance is called functional analysis or analysis of functions of dynamic processes. In Parsons' own definition:

Functional significance in this context is inherently teleological. A process or set of conditions either 'contributes' to the maintenance (or development) of the system or it is 'dysfunctional' in that it detracts from the integration, effectiveness, etc., of the system. It is thus the functional reference of all particular conditions and process *to the state of the total system as a going concern* which provides the logical equivalent of simultaneous equations in a fully developed system of analytical theory. This appears to be the only way in which dynamic *inter*dependence of variable factors in a system can be explicitly analysed without the technical tools of mathematics and the operational and empirical prerequisites of their employment.[30]

As a result, a third step is necessary to complete structural-functional analysis, that is, inclusion of a set of 'dynamic functional categories' which describe both, the important processes by which particular structures are maintained or upset and the relation of the system to its environment. They also must be complete to provide a logically adequate description of a concrete empirical system.

In summary, to quote a passage in which Parsons himself rather succintly summarizes the problem of structural-functional analysis as an alternate to dynamic analysis:

> If we have a sufficiently generalized system of categories for the systematic description and comparison of the structure of systems, then we have a setting within which we can mobilize our dynamic knowledge of motivational processes which are of significance in social system terms, the knowledge we possess is both fragmentary and of very uneven and unequal analytical status. The most effective way of organizing it for our purposes is to bring it into relation to a scheme of points of reference relative to the social system. This is where the much-discussed concept of 'function' comes in. We must, of course, 'place' a dynamic process structurally in the social system. But beyond that we must have a test of the significance of generalizations relative to it. That test of significance takes the form of the 'functional' relevence of the process. The test is to ask the question, what would be the differential consequences for the system of two or more alternative outcomes of a dynamic process? Such consequences will be found to fit into the terms of maintenance of stability or production of change, of integration or disruption of the system in some sense.[31]

Merton: The Problem of Structural Items and Their Consequences

Unlike Parsons, Merton is not so much concerned with the problem of dynamic analysis and its substitutes. His ideal of scientific theory is not necessarily that of viewing all phenomena as variables of one all-inclusive theoretical system.[32] He is more concerned with specifications of functional analysis in order to make it practically applicable to research.

Merton never gives a concise definition of functionalism. The central orientation of functionalism, he states, is expressed 'in the practice of interpreting data by establishing their consequences for larger structures in which they are implicated. . . .'[33] However, he never specifies adequately the 'larger structures'. They are 'a *range* of units for which the item has designated consequences', but this range may be 'individuals in diverse statuses, subgroups, the larger social system and culture systems'.

For Parsons, to have a complete and determinate picture of the total universe of functional analysis is of supreme importance, because on it hinges the entire problem of dynamic analysis. Merton, on the other hand, stressing practical research problems, leaves this important theoretical question unanswered. He sees difficulties involved in the determination of *one total* universe of functional analysis. He questions the assumption that the universe of functional analysis is always the social system as a whole: 'Whether cultural items do uniformly fulfil functions for the society viewed as a system and for all members of the society is presumably an empirical question of fact, rather than an axiom.'[34] Such objection may be valid. Yet, if there is to be functional analysis as defined above, some clear and independent system must be accepted as an assumption. This problem will be treated in more detail later, in connection with both the discussion of the concept of function and the discussion of the organismic model.

Merton's contribution to functionalism is his specification of certain concepts that provide a paradigm for functional analysis. They include primarily the concepts of items, functions, net balance of the aggregate of consequences, and functional alternatives. Perhaps the most characteristic element of Merton's functionalism is his emphasis on the items to which functions are imputed. In fact, his functionalism could be called item-centred in contrast to Parsons' system-centred functionalism.[35] According to him, items, comparable to Parson's structural categories, should be described 'as fully and as accurately as possible'.[36] He discusses in detail what should be included in the description of an item. In summary, it consists of:

1. Location of participants in the pattern within the social structure—differential participation;
2. Consideration of alternative modes of behaviour excluded by emphasis on the observed pattern (i.e., attention not only to what occurs but also to what is neglected by virtue of the existing pattern);
3. The emotive and cognitive meanings attached by participants to the pattern;
4. Distinction between the motivations for participating in the pattern and the objective behaviour involved in the pattern;
5. Regularities of behaviour not recognized by participants but which are nonetheless associated with the central pattern of behaviour.[37]

Yet, he admits that even this may be far from complete. The aim of this detailed description of items is to enable one to initiate functional research. It is the first and the most important step. Sheer description of a structural item, states Merton, provides a major clue to the functions performed by it: 'We suggest that the structural description of participants in the activity under analysis provides hypotheses for subsequent functional interpretations.'[38] The subsequent functional interpretation consists of showing the 'consequences' that the structural item has for specific social units.

The implication of Merton's notion of 'consequences' and the implications of his refusal to accept a 'social System' of the Parsonian type as a frame of reference for functional statements will be discussed in succeeding chapters.

Levy: Structural-Functional Requisite Analysis

Like Merton, Marion J. Levy, Jr. emphasizes as the first

step of structural-functional analysis a careful definition of the unit to which the analysis is applied. The unit in question is concrete rather than analytical, that is, it is a category which refers to cases which at least in theory are capable of physical separation from other cases of similar categories.[39] Thus, such categories or concepts as 'family', 'society', 'business firm' are concrete units in this sense. They are systems of social action involving a plurality of individuals; they identify membership units. As Levy explains,

> These units will not be defined as a collection of individuals of a given species but rather as the system of action that identifies such a collection and that does not 'exist' (i.e., is not empirically observable) in the complete absence of the plurality involved.[40]

Once a unit has been defined, the next step in the structural-functional analysis, according to Levy, is to assess the *setting* of the unit. By the term setting Levy means the 'factors that determine, either exactly or on a probability basis, the maximum range of possible variation in the patterns that characterize the unit'. Thus in the case of society in general as the unit of analysis, the setting consists of the factors of human heredity and nonhuman environment.

Levy's most significant contribution to functionalism, however, is his emphasis on precise conceptual distinctions, in particular his distinction between structural requisites, functional requisites, and structural and functional prerequisites. In fact, he calls his type of functionalism 'structural-functional requisite' analysis. The central problem in this analysis is discovering the implications of the existence of the unit under study within its setting.[41] That is, once the unit and its settings have been determined, two questions are to be asked: First, what operations must be done if such a unit is to exist in the given setting, and second, what uniformities or patterns of action must exist in terms of which such operations would be possible? The answer to the first question establishes the functional requisites of the unit, the answer to the second question establishes the structural requisites of the unit.

Levy's notion of functionalism differs from that of Merton by its emphasis not on the consequences of the unit under analysis, but on the conditions of its existence. Thus if the operation of the structure of a given unit is such that it either increases or maintains the unit's adjustment to its setting, the conditions of its existence or persistence are fulfilled. On the other hand, if this operation is such that the unit's adaptation to its setting is lessened through time, then the conditions of the unit's existence fail to be fulfilled, and the result is a change or dissolution of the unit as defined.[42] In this manner Levy has made the 'if, then' nature of functional analysis more explicit.

Levy emphasizes the phrase 'unit as defined'. As he explains, the fulfilment of the conditions of existence of the unit (eufunction) or lack of this fulfilment (dysfunction) is meaningful only in terms of the way the unit and its setting are conceived. Thus:

> A condition that is eufunctional from the point of view of a family group in one setting may conceivably be dysfunctional from a single member's point of view in that or another setting. Conditions that would be eufunctional for the American Communist Party under present conditions would undoubtedly be dysfunctional for modern United States society (if the latter is taken in its present form of private ownership of many, if not most, of the means of production), and so forth. Only reference to a particular unit *as defined on a particular level and to its setting* makes possible the classification of a condition or aspect of a condition as eufunctional or dysfunctional.[43]

Furthermore, Levy distinguishes between functional and structural prerequisites. This distinction is analogous to that of the requisites, but whereas the latter is basically a static distinction, the distinction of prerequisites takes the element of change into account. The focus of attention is on conditions that must pre-exist in time if a unit of a given type in its setting is either to come into being or to change in a particular way. Thus, the term 'functional prerequisite' is defined by Levy as 'a function (i.e., state of affairs resultant from the operation of a structure through time) that must pre-exist if a given unit in its setting is to come into being', whereas the term 'structural prerequisite' is defined as 'a structure (i.e., an observable uniformity of action or operation) that must pre-exist if a given unit in its setting is to come into being'.[44]

Levy, however, cautions that whenever a structure or a structural unit is undertaken as the subject of analysis, one must be clear as to what connotation is intended by the word structure. A clear distinction must be kept between concrete structures and analytic structures. Concrete structures are patterns of action which refer to units that are at least in theory capable of physical separation in time and/or space from other units of the same sort. Analytic structures, on the other hand, are patterned aspects of action that are not even theoretically capable of physical separation from other patterned aspects of action.[45] Thus a 'family', a 'business firm' are concrete structures because they refer to patterns which define distinct memberships, separable from other memberships of the same type. 'Economic' patterns, 'political' patterns, however, are analytic structures because there are no concrete acts that are totally devoid of either economic or political aspects. They are, therefore, aspects of action.

Analysis usually starts with some specific concrete structures and then proceeds to its analytic aspects in order to arrive at understanding of concrete structures on other levels of generalization. Thus, if some specific families are the original starting point of analysis, through consideration of their analytic structures, such as patterns of allocation of goods or patterns of authority distribution, one can arrive at an understanding of a structure on a higher level of generalization, say the American family. On the other hand, analysis may start with analytic structures and proceed to examination of the way in which the analytic structures are involved in concrete structures. One may start with consideration of equal distribution of authority and proceed to examine the way in which it is involved in the American family or, on a lower level of generalization, the way it is involved in some specific American families within specific time-space limitations.[46]

Levy cautions against confusion of the two types of structures especially in the analysis of change. Changes in concrete structures may be spoken of as causing changes in other concrete structures, but not so in the case of analytic structures. As Levy puts it:

> Patterns only analytically distinguished from the same concrete phenomenon cannot cause one another to do anything; both depend on the maintenance or change of the concrete phenomenon of which they are aspects. These changes may, of course, leave one aspect constant while others are changed. Many of the arguments as to whether economic or political factors cause one another cease to be problems when one no longer attempts to use analytic distinctions as though they were concrete ones and vice versa.[47]

In summary, Levy has attempted to specify in a conceptual manner both the character of the structures studied by functionalism and the character of the conditions for the existence of these structures within a larger structural setting.

Barber and Bredemeier: Problems of Interpretation

Both Bernard Barber and Harry Bredemeier have tried to clarify some of the misunderstandings as to the nature of functionalism.[48] Among these are the questions of whether functionalism is a method or a substantive theory, Levy's problem of functionalism as either abstract or concrete analysis, functionalism as either static or dynamic analysis, and finally the problem of the precise explanatory focus of functionalism. All these problems will be taken up later on in the study. Here they will be considered briefly, as stated by Barber and Bredemeier, only inasmuch as their treatment of these problems throws some light on the nature of functionalism.

Barber points out what has been accepted by functionalists ever since—that functionalism is in part a method of
analysing the relations among structural parts, and in part a
body of substantive sociological concepts and theory.
Insofar as it is a method of analysing social relations,
functionalism assumes that social systems are 'relatively
determinate, boundary-maintaining systems in which the
parts are interdependent in certain ways to preserve one
another and the character of the system as a whole'.[49] Such
an assumption, says Barber, can apply to many different
substantive systems. Hence, it is important that any particular piece of functional analysis should specify as explicitly as possible the substantive structural concepts it has
adopted so that they could be easily compared with alternative structural categories. For example, the concepts of
charismatic, traditional, and rational-legal authority can be
compared with those of democratic, autocratic, oligarchical
authority only when all of them are defined as explicitly as
possible.

Functionalists, of course, have used the method of
abstraction rather widely. Barber points out, however, that
there has been a tendency in functionalism to abstract one
variable aspect of concrete social reality to the exclusion of
other aspects and even to the exclusion of concrete social
reality as a whole. For example, as Tumin has pointed out,
Davis and Moore have abstracted one variable, the prestige
structure, from other structures in society, such as the family,
values, power, and, on the basis of this one, have attempted
to construct an abstract theoretic structural-functional
model. Furthermore, some functionalists have assumed that
although functionalism seeks to isolate the structural types
which are possible alternative solutions to any particular
functioning problem in society, at any given time in any
concrete social system only one structural type can be seen
best describing the particular system. This is not so, says
Barber—the isolation of different abstract structural types
should lead to the search for their 'possible intermixed,

but variously predominant' occurrence in a concrete society. As he explains:

> In the United States, the isolated nuclear type of family structure seems to be the predominant actually occurring type, but the extended type of family also occurs in this society under some specifiable conditions. For example, the extended type tends to persist among first-generation immigrants from peasant societies, among lower-class Negroes and among upper-class 'old' families.

Barber concludes that isolation of different abstract structural types and consequent examination of their relation to one another is necessary to a fruitful functionalist analysis of concrete societies and concrete processes within them.

One type of such processes is that of social change. Many commentators on functionalism have held that since functionalism assumes a concept of a boundary-maintaining system, such a concept implies the idea of 'closure', and hence functionalism is bound to remain static analysis, ill-equipped to study change. Barber points out that although closure is implied in the concept of system, it is only the temporary and provisional kind of closure characteristic of all scientific research. He states:

> Indeed, the assumption of structural-functional analysis is that it is necessary to understand the structure of a system at any moment in order to compare the system at different moments in a time series. Only by comparing different structures in a time series can one discover whether a system has manifested self-maintaining process or processes of change, short-term or long-term. How else can one define change except as transformation from one structural type to another structural type? Not all process is change for a large-scale or small-scale social system. Some process merely maintains the established structural type of the system.[49]

The problem of system-maintaining vs. system change raises the question whether this problem is the object of explanation in functionalism or whether the object is the origin and/or persistence of specific structures within the system. Harry C. Bredemeier was one of the first commentators on functionalism to clarify this question. According to him the two approaches must be clearly distinguished, but both of them are part of functional analysis. Functionalism tries to explain both the system and the structural elements implicated in the system. In the latter case a clear and systematic distinction must be always made between the question of origin of a structural element and the question of persistence of this element within a larger system. The question of origin can be handled by functionalism, but only by use of the special variant of functionalism found in evolutionary reasoning. That is, the structural elements of social systems can be seen as originating in the same manner as the structural traits of biological organisms—basically according to the principles of chance and the process of natural selection.

The question of persistence of structural elements within a system has to be approached in a different manner. Bredemeier's position is that it has to be conceptualized on the level of motives and attitudes. That is, the need which the structural element fulfils is to be interpreted in motivational terms. This, as will be discussed later, diverges from the more recent Parsonian position. But Bredemeier goes on to point out that it is not enough to ask 'what need does a structure satisfy?'; for a complete analysis one has to ask also 'what is the source of that need, i.e., what culture patterns give rise to that need?' Needs result from the normative definitions of the dominant culture.[50]

Bredemeier concludes by recommending a procedure for functional analysis. According to this procedure:

1. Productive analysis begins with a statement of the kind of action necessary to maintain some system of interrelationships, namely, the system of which the observed uniformity is a part.
2. It states the motivational conditions which are necessary to produce that action (the normative criteria of gratification which will yield the relevant action).

3. It describes the motivational patterns actually operating so as to produce the uniformity under analysis.
4. It seeks to find the source of these patterns (to isolate the normative criteria responsible for the observed actions).
5. It compares the consequences of the operating motivation with the motivations described as necessary, including the deviant modes of adjusting to frustration of efforts to meet the criteria in question.
6. It finally assesses the role played by the uniformity in question in contributing to the system of which it is a part.

Definition of Functionalism

On the basis of the above discussion we may now give a working definition of functionalism. The definition is broad enough to allow for the different emphases as presented in the above discussion but substantial enough to present a basis for a discussion of causal problems involved in functionalism. It can be said that:

> Functional analysis studies structural items of the social system in an attempt to show how they contribute toward integration or, inversely, disintegration of the system by either fulfilling or failing to fulfil some needs or sets of needs of the system, and in an attempt to show how these contributions bear on the existence of the item in the system.

Or briefly:

> Functional analysis studies the functions which a structural item of the social system has for the state of the system as a whole, and how these functions bear on the structural item itself.

MEANING OF CAUSALITY

For the purposes of this study, the term causality will connote a relation of determinacy between phenomena. That is,

> everything else is determined in accordance with laws by something else, this something else being the external as well as the internal conditions of the object in question.[51]

This means that phenomena have bearing or influence upon one another and that that influence is not haphazard or arbitrary, but on the contrary shows regularity and consistency.

The question whether all determinacy is causal is of no concern to this study. It suffices to accept that all causality is determinacy, and that causality permits of a number of types of determinacy.

Several epistemological positions will be assumed. First, the relation of determinacy between phenomena is assymmetrical. This probably is a widespread assumption among scientists, although many contemporary philosophers of science reject the notion of causality altogether. As Herbert Simon put it:

> In view of the generally unsavory epistemological status of the notion of causality, it is somewhat surprising to find the term in rather common use in scientific writing (when the scientist is writing about his science, not about its methodology). Moreover, it is not easy to explain this usage as metaphorical, or even as a carry-over of outmoded language habits. For, in ordinary speech and writing the causal relationship is conceived to be an assymmetrical one—an ordering—while 'functional relationship' and 'interdependence' are generally conceived as entirely symmetrical. When we say that *A* causes *B,* we do not say that *B* causes *A*; but when we say that *A* and *B* are functionally related (or interdependent), we can equally well say that *B* and *A* are functionally related (or interdependent). Even when we say that *A* is the independent variable in an equation, while *B* is the dependent variable, it is often our feeling that we are merely stating a convention of notation and that, by rewriting our equation, we could with equal propriety reverse the roles of *A* and *B*.[52]

Secondly, causation is an ontological reality rather than simply a mental category. N. S. Timasheff says:

> The source of the tension between experimentalists and methodologists is conspicuous: for the experimental scientists, causation 'means dependence of real things of nature on one

another', and does not refer to concepts including the mathematical ones. The elimination of causation from the number of the tools of scientific reasoning or the elimination, from causality, of the time dimension, is closely related to the ultramodernistic tendency to replace real phenomena by concepts. Some sixty years ago, with the appearance of K. Pearson's *Grammar of Science*, real phenomena started being replaced by 'routine sense impressions', now, sense impressions are being replaced by concepts. Conceptualism is, of course, one of the possible philosophical positions, just as is moderate realism, which underlies the work of the vast majority of the experimental scientists, or as is the thought processes and actions of ordinary men. Since, between concepts, there can be no causal relations, the modern conceptualists must eliminate the concept of causality. For the students of real phenomena, of referents and not of symbols, there is no obligation to follow suit.[53]

Furthermore, a distinction should be made between the ontological status of causality and the means of ascertaining it. Thus, such things as necessity, sufficiency, etc., called here characteristics of causality, will be considered as indices of determinacy relation between phenomena.

Finally, of the several possible types of causality, this study will consider two: *productive causality* and *telecausality*. More attention will be given to telecausality because it appears to be more prominent in functionalism, even though inadequately discussed in functionalist literature; more often it is simply dismissed as an illegitimate assumption.

The neologisms 'productive causality' and 'telecausality' may sound somewhat awkward, but there is need, especially in this area of causality, to make the meaning of the different types of causality precise. Thus, 'productive causality' refers to what in the Aristotelian terminology has been called efficient causality and in contemporary terminology just simply causality. In common usage, however, the adjective 'efficient' has really lost its original connotation of making or producing (*ex facere*). On the other hand, if the term 'causality' is used, as it is used here, in a generic sense, referring to different types of determinacy, then there must be other terms designating its specific meanings, in this case the meaning of production. Hence the writer feels that the simplest designation for this type of causality is 'productive causality'.

'Telecausality' refers to what is commonly known as teleology. But the meaning of teleology does not express the idea of causality. Since in this study teleology is considered to be a form of causality, then for the sake of precision this should be somehow expressed in the terminology. By derivation one can also use the word 'telecause,' whereas in the case of 'teleology' the phrase 'teleological cause' is somewhat awkward. The possible objection that the term 'telecausality' combines together words from two different languages is not a valid objection in view of the fact that there are so many terms which do the same, and yet are entered in the dictionaries, e.g., 'sociology,' 'culturology,' 'climatology,' etc. But why not 'finality' or 'final cause'? The word finality, like the word teleology in itself makes no reference to causation. Furthermore, the phrase 'final cause' or perhaps 'final causality' has a connotation of the ultimate end, and this is not necessarily involved in the presented intended meaning of the concept. Finally, the terms 'finality', 'final causes' to a great extent imply a reference to intention or purpose; but the notion of ends as used in this study does not necessarily involve this reference. In fact, this study emphasizes ends which are not intended by those in action. Thus the term 'telecausality' appears to the writer to be most appropriate under the circumstances.

GENERAL STATEMENT OF THE CAUSAL PROBLEM
IN FUNCTIONALISM

The basic logic of functional methodology can be briefly stated as follows:

x has the function of A for system y

In this statement, x refers to an item in the system or a property of the item, y refers to a self-persisting, boundary maintaining system, and A refers to the state of the system in terms of its 'need' satisfaction.

The basic causal question involved in this statement is whether it can be said that

$$x \text{ is a cause of } Ay$$

or

$$Ay \text{ is a cause of } x$$

This is the basic question of this study. The following pages will attempt to give an answer.

Chapter II

PRODUCTIVE CAUSALITY IN FUNCTIONALISM

The ontological meaning of productive causality is that of productivity—causation in the sense of production. To quote Mario Bunge:

> The reduction of causation to regular association as propounded by Humeans, amounts to mistaking causation for one of its tests; and such a reduction of an ontological category to a methodological criterion is the consequence of epistemological tenets of empiricism, rather than a result of an unprejudiced anaylsis of the laws of nature.
>
> What we need is a statement expressing the idea—common to both the ordinary and the scientific usage of the word—that causation, far more than a relation, is a category of genetic connection, hence of change, that is, a way of *producing* things, new if only in number, out of the other things.[1]

The basic question, however—how to ascertain productivity, still remains. When can it be said that one thing produces another? What is the test of productivity? Logical techniques, devised to ascertain productivity, involve a set of characteristics, so that the argument runs in this fashion: 'If these characteristics are present, there is productivity.'

LOGICAL FORMULATION OF THE PRINCIPLE OF PRODUCTIVE CAUSALITY

The most general formulation of the principle of productive causality can be stated thus: If x, then y, or if x is observed, then y is also observed. In this statement:

1. x is held to be the cause, y the effect, i.e., x produces y, according to our definition of causality.

2. x and y refer to classes of concrete phenomena, rather than to singular phenomena themselves; or, to classes of properties of the phenomena rather than the properties themselves.

3. Hence, x and y permit of greater or lesser abstractiveness.

4. The more abstract x or y, the more variables are covered by it. If a limited system of variables is assumed, the categories of x and y can be made relatively inclusive and thus reduce the number of unaccounted variables, and vice versa.

5. However, the more concrete x or y, the easier it is identifiable as a possible ontological cause or effect, but the more difficult it is to be certain of its actual causality or effectness; and vice versa, the more abstract x or y, the more difficult it is to identify it as a cause or effect, but the less difficult it is to ascertain logically its causality or effectness. (This is in one sense the problem of theory versus research.)

Characteristics of Productive Causality

The formula 'if x, then y' expresses two general characteristics, conditionalness and constant conjunction.

Conditionalness indicates emphasis on fulfilment of conditions necessary for occurrence of facts of a certain class, rather than on facts themselves. It ('if x') means that all conditions necessary for occurrence or effectiveness of x are satisfied. This, theoretically, may mean all other factors in the system or all subsystems of the system, since a subsystem is assumed to have a relative independence from the total system.

Constant conjunction means: if x, then y *always*. 'Always' means in all cases in the given universe of discourse.

However, this general notion of constant conjunction by itself does not show any productivity. It has to be specified.

Thus, productively causal constant conjunction involves the following characteristics:

1 *Sufficiency,* involving

A. *Adequacy:* occurrence of x is adequate for occurrence of y. Adequacy means that x contains in it that which makes y possible. This does not mean that x is the only adequate factor that makes y possible (this would be part of necessity); it means only that x contains in itself the things that make y possible even if other factors are also necessary for occurrence of y.

B. *Invariability:* if x occurs, y will occur invariably; upon occurrence of x, y will occur without exception.

11 *Necessity,* involving

A. *Uniqueness of bond:* there is a one-to-one correspondence between x and y; the existence of y follows (not necessarily in time) in a unique and unambiguous way from the existence of x. There is a single y for every x, and vice versa. In this way any cause other than x is eliminated. Thus: 'if x, and only x, then y', or 'no y without x, and only x'.

Unlike other characteristics of constant-conjunction and conditionalness, uniqueness is absent from other kinds of law, especially that of statistical regularities.

Uniqueness or *rigidity* of productive causality can be contrasted to the *souplasse* of statistical determination and plasticity of teleological determination in which a goal may be attained through a range of alternative means.[2]

B. *Continuity of action between cause and effect:* (closely related to uniqueness); absence of gaps in causal lines. Any discontinuity in causal chain would have to be assigned to the action of an extra cause; or, 'small causes have small effects'; or, 'if x, then y, and only y'.

When all the above mentioned characteristics are present, then we may say that there is productive causality between x and y, i.e., x productively causes y, or rather, x produces y.

The logical formulation of the principle of productive causality can be summarized as follows:

If x, and only x, happens, then and only then y, and only y, is without exception produced by it.[3]

PRODUCTIVELY CAUSAL CHARACTERISTICS IN FUNCTIONALISM

The question of productive causality in functionalism is relevant only to the case of an item or its property in a system producing a state of the system, not inversely. That is, it applies to the case 'x produces Ay' rather than 'Ay produces x'. It is the question of whether the basic functional statement 'x has the function of A for the system y' could be in any way interpreted as 'x in some way *produces A* in the system y.' The question is the same for both microfunctionalism and macrofunctionalism. Thus, in the statement that specificity-neutrality orientation is functional for the doctor-patient system of relations, can we say that the specificity-neutrality orientation productively causes the functioning of the system, or in the statement that the social system is a function of the pattern-maintenance subsystem, can we say that the functioning of the pattern-maintenance subsystem productively causes the functioning of the social system?

The presence of the characteristics of productive causality in functionalism can be summarized as follows:

Characteristic:	*In Functionalism:*
conditionalness	present
adequacy	present
invariability	present
uniqueness of bond	absent
continuity of action	absent

That functionalism attempts explanation of the 'if-then' variety is obvious upon examination of its basic principles, viz., relating of parts of the system to the needs of the system. Inasmuch as it provides an explanation, however, it assumes that the explananses are adequate to account for the explanandum. If the phrase 'x is functional for the state of the system y,' means that x contributes to the maintenance or disturbance of the system y, then what is inescapably implied is that x is able to provide for the system y what it needs to maintain itself. Adequacy is implied in the notion of function itself, just as lack of adequacy is implied in the notion of dysfunction.

To put it another way, however, adequacy is implied in functionalism inasmuch as functionalism is a form of what has been called 'deductive nomological explanation,' i.e., explanation through deduction from general laws. Accordingly, x can be said to warrant Ay because Ay can be deduced from general laws under which x can be subsumed. Thus, if $L_1, L_2 \ldots L_n$ are general laws involved in functionalism, such as, for example, the generalization that for a social system to function properly its prerequisites or needs must be met, and x is an empirically observed item that can be said to satisfy the system's needs, then the conclusion that x contributes to the functioning of the system y follows. Thus:

$$\text{if } L_1, L_2 \ldots L_n$$
$$\text{and } x$$
$$\text{then } Ay$$

where Ay follows logically from the major and the minor premise.[4]

For example, in his study of the medical profession, Parsons is interested in the normative patterns which are functional for the system of doctor-patient relationships. But any system of relations can be functionally maintained only if there are institutionalized mechanisms which meet the requirements (or needs) of the system of relations in question (general law assumed.) Any system of doctor-patient relations requires that there be an access to the patient's body, yet an access to it and communication about it without undue discomfort or embarrassment (a more specific generalization or law assumed, applicable only to doctor-patient relations). Now, Parsons shows that the normative patterns of specificity and effective-neutrality can be subsumed under these general laws, that they provide a concrete instance of mechanisms which meet the requirements of the doctor-patient interaction system. Hence, his conclusion is that the patterns of specificity and affective-neutrality are functional for this system. This provides for Parsons an adequate explanation of the system's functioning. An adequate explanation means adequacy of the explanans in the sense defined above, because the general laws through which the explanation is achieved are implicated in the attested explanans. As Hempel says, 'A nomological explanation shows that we might in fact have *predicted* the phenomenon at hand (functional maintenance of doctor-patient relations, in our case), if at an earlier time we had taken cognizance of the facts stated in the explanans.'[5] Thus, recognition of what the patterns of specificity and affective-neutrality mean makes it possible to say that in any system of social relations in which these patterns occur, discomfort and embarrassment will be reduced inasmuch as the interaction will refer only to very pertinent points, and therefore feelings, emotions and ego involvement will be controlled.

The generalization involved in functionalism contains two further aspects: (1) generalization about recurrences in time, and (2) generalization about the type of the explananses. The first aspect is the question of invariablity, the second, that of uniqueness of bond or the question of functional alternatives.

Hempel points out that the predictive power of a nomological explanation, because its explanans contains general laws, permits prediction of recurrences of the phenomenon described in its conclusion. That is, the laws $L_1, L_2 \ldots L_n$ involved in the above explanation imply that Ay will recur whenever and wherever x is realized, all other things being equal. In the case of functionalism, 'all other things' involve the interdependence of x with all the other variables of the system; but this does not change the situation in regard to the invariability of x.

In Parsons' sociology admission of general laws was a slow process. As Devereux points out, although Parsons had always tried to talk in terms of general analytical theory, his indebtedness to Max Weber kept him busy in comparative studies of institutions as they were embedded in one or another culture. His 'insistence that the relevant socio-cultural context be always taken into account threatened continually to ensnare him in the sort of cultural relativity and historicism of which he accused the idealists.'[6] In fact Parsons' famous pattern-variables, though they made up part of his attempt to build a generalized theory of social action, turned out, in the *Social System*, to be little more than classificatory devices for descriptive analysis of different social institutions within a specific cultural context.[7] It is in Parsons' new synthesis, the four functional problem schema, that the pattern-variables acquire their full significance as variables of a generalized theory applicable across cultural contexts.[8]

In any case, the new Parsonian synthesis makes generalized laws of the widest scope part and parcel of functional analysis. By the same fact it assumes invariability in the sense explained above.

The second aspect of generalization, regarding the type of the explanans, and involving the question of the uniqueness of bond between the explanans and the explanandum, has been posing a very interesting problem for functionalism. Functionalists of both the sociological and anthropological extraction have discussed this problem under the title of functional alternatives. Both Parsons and Merton took a position against Malinowski's functional indispensability, and it can be said that today most functionalists admit the possibility of functional alternatives. As Merton put it, 'Just as the same (structural) item may have multiple functions, so may the same function be diversely fulfilled by alternative items. . . . There is a range of variation in the structures which fulfil the function in question.'[9] Or to quote Johnson:

> No mechanism is indispensable to a social system. That is to say, we can always conceive of the system achieving its goals and meeting its needs without that particular mechanism, for some other mechanism might have the same function. It is perhaps rare for a social system to depend upon one mechanism alone to fulfill a given need. There are usually functionally 'equivalent' mechanisms. For example, in polygynous marriages . . . the danger of jealousy or rivalry between the wives of the same man is fairly great. There is, then, a 'need' in such systems for mechanisms that will forestall or reduce disruption due to jealousy or rivalry. . . . There are at least five such mechanisms (hierarchy of authority among the wives, husband's obtaining the wife's consent before taking another wife, sororal polygyny, separate housing for each wife and her children, husband's rotation among his wives). Some of them are found together in the same society. Others are to some extent 'alternatives'. To cite a few more examples, hereditary monarchs can be dispensed with as long as it is possible to elect chiefs of state. Elected judges can be substituted for appointive judges, or *vice versa*.[10]

We must therefore conclude that the manner in which most contemporary functionalists view their methodology denies any uniqueness of bond between the functional explanans and the functional explanandum. However, the problem is far from being solved. In fact, some functionalists who have admitted the existence of functional alternatives have had second thoughts. Thus Johnson says:

> The existence of functional alternatives is too obvious to dwell on. Yet we are obliged to recognize that such expressions as 'equivalent mechanisms' and 'functional alternatives' are somewhat loose. Every social structure imposes some limits on the structural innovations that would be compatible with it . . . Moreover, two different mechanisms might not fulfil the same need to the same degree. The relative merits of elected and appointed judges, for example, have been debated. In any case, the threats to appointive systems are somewhat different from those in elective systems. . . . Finally, . . . any partial structure

may have both functions and dysfunctions, for different needs of the social system. It is probably rare for any two 'equivalent' mechanisms to have exactly the same complete set of functional and dysfunctional consequences.[11]

Perhaps the question of functional indispensability is not really an either-or question; a question of admitting it or denying it. One wonders if it would be possible to have any explanation at all if an indefinite number of alternative explananses were to be assumed. Obviously, if one explanans were to be always as good as any other, the entire explanation would not be much more than sophistry. On the other hand, if no functional alternatives whatsoever were to be admitted in any other way than the one observed, then the entire explanation would really not be much more than mere description. If a joking relationship between a man and his in-laws functions to maintain friendly relations between the two parties within a specific society and nothing else can perform this function in this society, then an adequate description of this joking relationship would be tantamount to an adequate description of friendly relations between the two parties.

If friendly relations between the two parties mean joking relations between them, then instead of superimposing our culture-bound concept of 'joking' relations on this pattern of behaviour it would be more objective to drop this term altogether, and call this pattern just simply normal friendly relations between the two parties in the specific culture, since this is by assumption the only way 'normal', 'equilibrating' relations take place between them. Thus, adequate explanation is reduced to adequate description and functional method becomes nothing more than a method of nominal definitions (in terms of our Western culture-bound terms) of different behaviour patterns within specific cultures.

The functionalist sociologists today most probably would not subscribe to either extreme. They would deny the possibility of unlimited alternatives but equally would deny absolute functional indispensability of specific structural items.[12]

The question of functional alternatives is related to the question of the level of generalization of system needs and at the same time it remains an empirical problem. If the need which a specific structural item satisfies is conceived in very general terms, then this generality will permit a greater number of possible substitutes for the item. Thus, if joking relations between the in-laws fulfil the need for friendly, stable relations between the two, then possible substitutes for joking relations could be many, all other things in the given social structure allowing it. On the other hand, if it fulfils a need, let us say, of status equalization between the two parties, then the number of possible substitutes obviously will be reduced.

But the ultimate test of indispensability of specific structural items remains an empirical one. Only empirical study can give certitude (even if it is one of increased probability) that a specific structural item is either dispensable or indispensable. In any case, much more study of the question of functional alternatives is necessary. What becomes clear, however, is that the question of productive causality in functionalism involves both the problem of generalization and the problem of certitude.

We turn, finally, to the question of continuity of action in functionalism. In the functional method, x performs a function of A for y, x is never considered to be an altogether independent variable. On the contrary, it is always seen as interdependent with other variables. Hence the Ay is never seen as a resultant of nothing but x. It is a resultant of a network of variables together with x. The variable x is only a part of the whole and a part of a whole does not produce the whole. Thus, it is never if x, then Ay, and only Ay, but it might be if x, then z, if z, then k, and if x, z, k, then Ay.

In his study of social change in the industrial revolution, Neil Smelser relates the values of Nonconformity to the breakdown of the old eighteenth century 'putting out' cotton industry and to the development of the factory system. His explanation is typically functional. He is careful to emphasize that the relationship between the two is not causal; there have been other factors associated with the change. The values of Nonconformity, therefore, appear in his study as 'legitimizers' of behaviour, or 'criteria' of judgement of the old system of behaviour *vis-a-vis* the possibilities of a new system. Thus:

> The manufacturing districts partook heavily of the Methodist revival and the associated invigorating Noncomformity. This is to assert neither that Dissent caused the industrial revolution nor that incipient economic development caused Nonconformity to be revitalized. . . . It is sufficient that there existed, in substantial strength, certain *criteria* whereby bottlenecks in the existing industrial structure were deemed unsatisfactory on the one hand, and whereby motivation to modify this structure was encouraged on the other. Methodism and the other branches of Dissent seem clearly to fulfil this requirement in the late eighteenth century.[13]

If there is anything that functionalism negates almost by design, it is precisely the continuity of action between any single structural item and the total state of the functional system.[14] Multiple causality is an implicit assumption of functionalism. To this we will turn our attention presently.

To conclude, of all the characteristics of productive causality, functionalism involves only the sufficiency aspect, but lacks the necessity aspect. From the strict point of view of productive causality therefore, functionalism has not progressed very much beyond correlative analysis. It goes beyond pure correlative analysis, however, on two accounts:

1. Pure correlative analysis, besides conditionalness, involves only invariability, but not adequacy; functionalism involves both.

2. Functionalism specifies the system within which the correlates occur. This limits the number of correlates; some

of them are treated as constants, and thus productive causation is made more possible.

'INTERCAUSALITY' IN FUNCTIONALISM

From a less rigid point of view, ascertaining causation is a matter of degree of possibility (probability included) that all the characteristics of the causal bond are present. The more the variables within a system are limited and the more their correlative relation to each other is defined, the more probability there is that a variable will be a productive cause of a state of the system in which it appears.[15]

Thus if a variable x could be said to be in any way a productive cause of some state of a subsystem a, and if the state of the total system Ay is assumed to be a result of the states of its subsystems; if the subsystems are specified, for example, a, b, c, d,—then we can say that x, assuming b, c, d, are operative, is in an indirect way a productive cause of the state of the total system Ay. This, not through any necessity between x and Ay, but sufficiency and necessity assumed between a, b, c, d, and Ay. Thus:

if x produces Aa

and Aa, Ab, Ac, Ad produce Ay (by definition)

then x, if b, c, d, present, produces indirectly Ay

The assumptions made in this argument are (1) that x can be determined to be a productive cause of Aa, and (2) that none of the subsystems a, b, c, d, by themselves are sufficiently and necessarily connected with Ay, but all of them together. The second assumption suggests the idea of intercausality; the first, that of precipitant causality. Thus we introduce the notion of *intercausality* and, connected with it, MacIver's notion of *precipitant causality*. Both of these seem to be involved in functionalism.

As to the first assumption, subsystem a is treated the same way as the system y, i.e., the more the variables are limited and specified, the greater the probability of productive causation between them and the state of the system. The point here is that—although strictly speaking it might not be possible to demonstrate productive causality in this case—if the variables of the system are limited and specified enough, the probability of productive causality between any single variable and the state of the system, provided the other variables are present, is such that in practice we often speak or imply such relationships to be productively causal.

An instructive example in this respect is William Whyte's by now famous study of friction which occurs along the flow of work in the restaurant. Attempting to explain this friction, Whyte related the 'smoothly working' conditions to the restaurants in which indirect, impersonal patterns of communication between the waitresses and the countermen prevailed, while he related the 'friction' conditions to the restaurants in which the waitresses communicated personally with the countermen. As a good functionalist, Whyte never says that there is a causal bond between these structural patterns and the working state of the restaurants. The latter depends upon many other patterns too, and Whyte mentions a few: differentiation of roles, other communication systems, supervision, etc. The relation between the patterns in question and the state of the restaurant systems is explained through the need assumed to be operative in our society, that is, the need for those of higher status, in this case men, to originate action for those of lower status, in this case, women. Thus, the patterns whereby the waitresses give direct, person to person orders to the countermen frustrate this need—and hence friction. On the other hand, in the restaurants where the order-giving by the waitresses has been made quite impersonal, barring direct conctact between them and the countermen, frustration of this need has been avoided—and hence harmonious working relations.

Although Whyte never says that he has isolated the cause of friction in the restaurant relations he studied, for practical purposes the pattern of waitresses personally and directly ordering the work of the countermen can be considered as such. First of all, the logic of Whyte's argument is that of the traditional method of causal analysis, the *method of difference*. Thus, both the restaurants with friction and the restaurants without friction were assumed to have basically the same structure, except for the patterns of relations between the waitresses and the countermen. The restaurant without friction included a pattern of impersonal and indirect ordering of the countermen by the waitresses, whereas the restaurant with friction involved a pattern of personal and direct ordering. Hence the latter was suggested as the explanans of friction. Secondly, Whyte assumed other structural patterns to be functioning adequately enough as not to be significantly related to the friction in the flow of work. This assumption is quite reasonable in view of Whyte's description and specification of the structure of both types of restaurants and in view of the differences found in only one structural variable, that of waitress-countermen relations. Thus, in practice, the type of the waitress-countermen relations can be considered as productive of either harmonious or frictional functioning of the restaurants in question, even if it cannot be said for certain that it is both the necessary and the sufficient condition of such functioning. But, if we can assume that relatively all significant components of the restaurant social structure have been specified and that only one of them can be shown by experimental technique to be related to friction, then the probability of its being the necessary and sufficient condition of friction is high enough for it to be considered and dealt with as the precipitant cause.

Similar logic is involved in Parsons' discussion of the modern medical profession. As in Whyte's work, the crucial procedure of Parsons's study is the method of difference. Parsons employs what has been called a *Gedankenexperiment*. He studies the established normative patterns of doctor-patient relationships by asking what would be the consequences for the system of such relationships of some imagined deviation from this established pattern. Thus, system-maintaining consequences are related to the established norm pattern of functional specificity, affective neutrality, universalism, group-orientation, and performance, while system-disruptive consequences are related to the opposite of the established patterns, those functionally diffuse, affective, particularistic, self-oriented, quality directed. It is imagined that the system in which the disruptive consequences take place has the same elements as the established system except for the patterns of either specificity or neutrality, or universalism, or group-orientation, or performance. The causal effectiveness of these becomes more probable inasmuch as by definition there are only two possibilities for each of the patterns, either diffuseness or specificity, either affectivity or affective neutrality, either particularism or universalism, either self-orientation or collectivity orientation, either emphasis on quality or on performance. Since through the imaginative experiment only one side of these five sets can be shown to be associated with harmonious doctor-patient relations, deviations from any one of these into the opposite direction can be considered for practical purposes as producing a disruption of the system because the others, due to their interrelatedness with it, would not be able to function properly.

These few examples show that a basic method involved in functional studies is that of experimental inquiry, which, of course, is also the method of productively causal investigation. MacIver explains the formula of productively causal investigations thus:

> We identify the situation or type of situation in which the phenomenon occurs, as against a comparable situation or type of situation from which it is absent, and engage ourselves to discover how the phenomenon is related to the differential organization of the situation containing it. If X is the specific difference and it is found within the situation or conjecture C we proceed to the consideration of C_1, the comparable situation or conjecture lacking X.[16]

It is possible to phrase the logic of functional studies in the same way. We identify the state of the system in which an item occurs and compare it with a state of the system in

44

which the item does not occur. If X is some pattern of behaviour within a system of patterns of behaviour S, we describe X as functional for S if it is implicated only in S and not S_1, a different state of the system. On the other hand, we call X as dysfunctional for S if it can be seen as implicated in S_1 rather than S. It should be noted that S_1 is always a hypothetical system in reference to S, i.e., a state of the system which is not assumed to exist empirically, but which is inferred or imagined as either lacking or implicating X. But in spite of the same method, the difference between the pure productively causal analysis and pure functional analysis lies precisely in that the former attempts to determine both necessity and sufficiency of a variable in the sense described above, whereas the latter by definition excludes necessity. That is, the former looks for the independent variable, whereas for the latter, by definition, there are no independent variables. The loss, however, is compensated by the gain in that all variables are specified in the system, and hence all of them together supply the necessity aspect.

This brings us to the second assumption of our argument, namely, that of the legitimacy of assuming a system of limited interdependent variables as the logical framework of explanation. A discussion of this question will be presented later on in this study. Here it will suffice to say that the virtue of assuming a theoretical model of explanation lies precisely in this, that by definition all the basic variables of the system are identified, though in a very generalized form. Thus, for example, Parsons' model of the system made up of the four functional subsystems assumes, by definition, that the four subsystems are sufficient and necessary for the functioning of the total system.

However, if functionalism involves an intercausal analysis, the claim that a variable in the intercausal system can be considered as a precipitant productive cause assumes that the variable, albeit its interdependence with other variables, is nevertheless in some way independent from them. That is, at least at the time when we consider the variable as a precipitant cause, the functioning of the other variables must be more dependent upon it than it is dependent upon them. It will be worthwhile to quote MacIver on this point:

> The act or event we single out as the precipitant is still inextricably bound up with respect alike to its own initiation and to its causal operation, with the whole moving dynamic system. It would be meaningless to define the precipitant as that without which the change would not have taken place. Without any one of a thousand things and without the express interaction of them all the change would not have taken place. On this ground we might even deny that what we have called the precipitant has any more causal significance than any of the numerous other factors involved.
>
> But the fact that numerous other conditions are equally *necessary* for the result affords no ground for the denial of the distinctive role of the precipitant.[17]

Further, MacIver explains that although all conditions are necessary, and we may add sufficient in view of the system assumption, it does not follow that they are equally important for our understanding of a *particular* phenomenon at a particular time. At the particular time some of these conditions or variables become instrumental to others, and those which are less instrumental are more causally precipitant.

In regard to functionalism, first, a relative independence of the functional subsystems is assumed by Parsons. Each subsystem is held to have functional problems and hence subsystems of its own. All systems and subsystems are assumed to be boundary-maintaining. 'A boundary', says Parsons, 'means simply that a theoretically and empirically significant difference between structures and processes internal to the system and those external to it exists and tends to be maintained'.[18] This does not mean that the analytical systems exist as differentiated systems empirically but it implies that there is a possibility of such empirical differentiation along the analytical boundaries, since the analytical distinction implies a functional basis in empirical reality. Hence, the concrete structural subsystems can be seen as corresponding *primarily* to one or another functional analytical subsystem. In relation to economy Parsons says that 'it is inherent that the analytical boundaries will correspond to the lines of differentiation between concrete roles and collectivities most closely in those societies which are in general highly differentiated and which stress the economic aspects of their structure and functioning'.[19] Thus, business firms, though not exclusively economic organizations, nevertheless *primarily* are units in the adaptive system, just as families, although partly economic and partly integrative and partly involved in the goal-attainment subsystem of the society, are primarily units in the pattern-maintenance subsystem.[20]

Alvin Gouldner has drawn attention to the significance of Parsons' distinction between interdependence and independence of parts, but has also indicated that functionalism must go even further and make an attempt to assess the varying degrees of independence of the social system's parts. He writes:

> In *Structure of Social Action,* Parsons has stressed that independent parts are also interdependent, he has tended to treat both independence and interdependence as 'constants' rather than as variables. We, on the contrary, have emphasized that they are variables. To say that two parts are interdependent is not to imply that they are equally so and thus, even with a system of interdependent parts, various parts can have *varying* degrees of independence or freedom.
>
> Having gone this far, it is now evident that a stress on the 'web of interdependence' within a system by no means relieves the analyst of the problem of factor weighing or loading. The analyst must still cope with the task of determining the differential contribution made by different system parts to the state of the system as a whole. In short, different system parts make different degrees of contribution to either the stability or the change of the system, and these need to be analytically and empirically distinguished.[21]

47

To sum up, it is possible to see functionalism as productively intercausal analysis involving precipitant causality. This means that any variable in the social system can be seen as a true productive cause, provided all the other variables specified in the total system can be assumed to be functioning. But at any given time some variables are more independent than others. These more independent variables inasmuch as they contribute to the state of the system can be said to be precipitantly causal of that state. Attesting this is the fact that functionalist studies employ the logic of scientific experiment. In doing this they single out one or a few variables of the system as being of strategic importance for the state of the system and at the same time, at least for the purposes of the study, assume all other variables to be nonproblematic. Although the singled out variables are not considered to be both sufficient and necessary for the production of the specific state of the system, nevertheless to the degree all the other variables can be determined to depend upon them—to that degree they become necessary for the system. As Gouldner has pointed out, one weakness of functionalism has been precisely the fact that it never took enough pains to determine the various degrees of dependence and independence of the variables within the assumed systems. This, nevertheless, remains the task of the functional studies, if they are to become more precise and more scholarly, even if less sensational.

THE PROBLEM OF PRODUCTIVE CAUSALITY IN PARSONS' CRITIQUE OF MAX WEBER

Parsons continually emphasizes that on the question of Protestant ethics being the cause of the development of capitalism, the critics of Max Weber have misunderstood him. The critics have claimed that Max Weber ignored any causes other than the Protestant Ethic, that he failed to see that the Protestant Ethic itself was related to the 'material' factors in the development of capitalism. Parsons explains that Max Weber neither was unaware of other factors in the development of capitalism, nor considered the Protestant Ethic as something free-floating, unrelated to other conditions of the time. But he points out that Weber's main concern was to show that the Protestant Ethic was a cause of the development of capitalism in the West without which it simply would not have come about. Not that there were no other causes, causes relatively independent of the Protestant Ethic, and probably just as important, as for instance, modern science, a rationalized legal system, rational bureaucratic administration in the state, etc.; but from the historical point of view the Protestant Ethic was of crucial importance on two accounts, because it preceded the other factors in time, and because it could be shown that in societies other than those of Western Europe, where very often the other factors were present but lacking that of religion with an ethic similar to that of Protestantism, capitalism did not develop. To interpret Weber's work as an attempt to establish that only religious elements were important both in the development of the Protestant Ethic and in the development of capitalism, according to Parsons, is to go against the fundamental position of Weber's sociology, that of the voluntaristic theory of action instead of an idealistic theory of emanation.[22] Parsons points out that to understand Weber's argument properly one has to understand the ideal type method employed by Weber. Accordingly, the Protestant Ethic of Weber's analysis is not a concrete individual phenomenon but is an abstraction referring to a combination of features of actions of an indefinite plurality of concrete individuals. (This combination of features is not claimed to have actually existed as a unit, i.e., the abstraction is not to be reified.) This is one basic aspect of the ideal type method. But the actions of concrete individuals include other features as well, in this case, features that can be subsumed under concepts other than that of the Protestant Ethic. In the genesis of capitalism all these features complemented one another and have to be seen as interdependent.

Thus Parsons takes pains to show that for Max Weber the relation of the ethics of ascetic Protestantism to the spirit of capitalism, in spite of the 'congruence' between the two, is not one of *logical* consequences of the set of religious ideas for practical conduct based on them. On the contrary, the relation between the two itself has to be seen in the light of the practical attitudes and everyday interests of the masses. Hence it is more psychological than logical, involving intricacies of mutual interdependence, rather than simple logical deduction. As Parsons says:

> First, the relevant consequences (of the religious ideas on practical conduct) are, as . . . (Weber) puts it, 'psychological' rather than purely logical. The logical consequences operate, but not alone; they must be taken in conjunction with the constellation of interests involved, which may, as between two equally possible logical alternatives, bias action in the direction of one, or even inhibit the development of the full logical consequences in certain other directions.
>
> Secondly, the influence of a system of religious ideas on practical attitudes is to be regarded as a real process in time, not a static logical deduction. In the course of it the system of ideas itself may undergo change. In fact . . . the Protestant attitude toward economic acquisition underwent a steady process of change, and it was only in the later stages that the full consequences relevent in the present context emerged. Above all Weber insists that the original Reformers themselves were by no means filled with the spirit of capitalism. Their concern was solely religious and they would have sharply repudiated the attitudes taken by their successors. But this does not in the least disprove that these later attitudes were in an important degree the consequences of the religious ideas put forward by the Reformers.[23]

Thus, says Parsons, Max Weber's method of assessing the causal significance of the Protestant Ethic in the genesis of capitalism not only does not ignore other factors, but, on the contrary, takes into account their interdependence with religious ethics. In fact, it can be said that in spite of the dangers of distortions of the concrete historical phenomenon, Weber chose the ideal type method in order to unravel the intricacies of intercausal relations of factors determining action. Very instructive in this respect is Parsons' critique of Sorokin's criticism of Max Weber. Sorokin, in a very short passage, criticizes Weber for attempting to assess productive causation between Protestantism and capitalism. He says that Weber admits that in the genesis of the economic ethic associated with capitalism the religious factor is only one of many possible ones, as for instance, geographical, historical, physical and psychological factors. Hence, says Sorokin,

> granting that Weber's analysis of the effects of the *Wirtschaftsethik* on economic life is accurate, we in no way can ascribe these effects to religion (A) only because the factor of the *Wirtschaftsethik* is a complex embodiment of numerous and various factors (B, C, D, E, F,) which shape it.[24]

From this he concludes that:

> Weber's analysis does not show even tentatively what the share of the religious factor is in moulding the *Wirtschaftsethik*, and correspondingly, its share in conditioning the effects of the *Wirtschaftsethik* in the field of economic phenomena. Thus, after Max Weber's work we are as ignorant about the degree of efficiency in the religious factor as we were before.[25]

Parsons criticizes Sorokin for this conclusion. First of all he points out that Max Weber never meant to ascribe the effects of the economic ethic on economic life to religion only, and secondly, he shows that in his criticism Sorokin has measured Weber's work by a standard altogether inapplicable to it. It is in principle impossible, says Parsons, to assess exact quantitative importance of ideal-type units. Weber's judgment as to the influence of Protestantism on capitalism

> is not a judgment of exact quantitative importance in percentage terms—such a judgment would be absurd. It does, however, say a great deal about the degree of efficiency of this

factor—that without it the historical development would certainly have been radically different.[26]

The logic of Weber's study is the logic of intercausal analysis. It is not a question of proportional contribution of factors; it is rather the problem of accordant contribution of factors, i.e., each factor is a cause and produces the phenomenon in question, provided all the others are present. When seen from the point of view of time sequence, this type of causality becomes *precipitant* causality, and it is apparently in this sense that Max Weber considers the causal efficacy of the Protestant Ethic.

It is noteworthy that while Parsons stresses that Max Weber was very much aware of other factors in the production of capitalism and never held the Protestant Ethic to be the sole factor, yet he takes pains to show that Weber's work successfully demonstrates that the Protestant Ethic was causal of capitalism, Sorokin, on the other hand, criticizes Max Weber precisely for claiming the Protestant Ethic to be causal of capitalism, yet evaluates Weber's study as logically functional in character. It is obvious that for Sorokin functional analysis and causal analysis are exclusive of one another.[27] Parsons never takes up the question explicitly, but equally he never explicitly closes the door to a discussion of this problem. In fact, analysis of Weber's study, as was shown here, implicitly assumes a significant connection between the two.

Chapter III

TELECAUSALITY IN FUNCTIONALISM

THE QUESTION OF TELEOLOGY IN FUNCTIONALIST LITERATURE

On the whole, contemporary functionalists say very little about telecausality or rather teleology in functional analysis. If they do talk about it, they talk about it with a good deal of embarassment and, by and large, take either of two positions; they either admit that the question of teleology is pertinent to functionalism and leave it at that, or they deny its real pertinence and attempt to point out that either the teleological meaning in functionalism is purely figurative since all functional propositions can be expressed non-teleologically, or that its meaning is not the traditional meaning, i.e., teleology in the sense of the individual's purpose or aim.

Parsons states at one point that functionalism has an inherently teleological significance inasmuch as it views processes of the social system as either contributing to its maintenance or development or detracting from its integration and effectiveness.[1] Parsons' meaning of teleology here is not that of the motives or purposes of the individual actor, but rather that of the end of action itself, *finis operis* rather than *finis operantis*. Most of the commentators on teleology in functionalism refer to it in this sense. In other words, the question of finality in functionalism is not one of ends or motives of the individuals, but one of the ends of the system of action itself, regardless of the motives of the individuals participating in it.[2] It is in this sense also that telecausality will be considered in this study. Yet, critics of teleology in functionalism agree that this is methodologically inadmissable. To hold that there are ends in the social system which are independent of those of the individuals participating in it is, according to them, an illegitimate transferal of concepts. Thus Tima-sheff says that extension of the meaning of functionalism to cover teleology is not necessary and a functionalist may remain on safe grounds by confining himself to answering questions about contributions of parts to wholes and about integration of the social system as a whole.[3] Along similar lines, Dorothy Emmet has pointed out that in biology, the first discipline to deal with the problems of functionalism, the question of teleology has been shifting more and more to the question of the endurance of the functional wholes.[4]

H. C. Bredemeier has pointed out that there has been much confusion between the type of functional explanation which focuses on contributions of parts to the whole and the type which tries to explain the persistence of parts by the contribution they make to the whole. He states that the only way the latter type of explanation can be made empirically testable is when it is formulated in such a manner that reference is made to the motivations of the participating individuals. Thus, in the functional hypothesis that the Hopi Rain Dance performs the latent function for the Hopi of reinforcing the group identity by providing a periodic occasion on which the scattered members of the group assemble to engage in a common activity, it is not clear whether we are to understand the hypothesis as stating that the ceremonies are held because the participants derive some gratification from them (motivational explanation), or whether it states that they are held because they contribute to group survival (telecausal explanation on the group level). If the latter interpretation is intended, says Bredemeier, then no empirical test of the hypothesis is possible. Hence,

Bredemeier advocates that functional analysis be reformulated in such a way as to include motivational analysis. He concludes:

> A thorough (functional) analysis involves asking *both* what are the consequences of the given pattern, *and* what are the conditions that make these consequences functional? The answer to the latter question must always be sought in terms of the normative orientations and symbolic definitions comprising individuals' motivations.[5]

In a similar manner Harry M. Johnson involves functionalism in motivational analysis. But he goes even further by showing a close relationship between motives and functions. As if trying to salvage teleology for functionalism, he points out that motives and functions often converge. Making reference to Homans' and Schneider's study of unilateral cross-cousin marriages, Johnson asks a double question: First, what motives might be involved in the marriages of the type in which the young man marries his mother's brother's daughter, and second, what functions does such a matrilateral cross-cousin marriage perform? His answer is that as far as motives are concerned, the groom as well as all the people involved in the marriage, under the circumstances in which they are all placed, assume rather naturally that this type of marriage will work out for the young couple and for the relations between their parental families. In regard to function, the answer is similar. Under the circumstances, the function of this type of marriage is to stabilize the marriage in the situation made difficult by the circumstances, and to strengthen the ties between somewhat distant families. Johnson concludes that motives and latent functions are not far apart and suggests that perhaps latent functions are really institutionalized motives.[6]

Not all critics of functionalism, however, would solve the problem of teleology in functionalism by reference to the motives of the participants. Many of them would rather keep the question of motives and that of functions as two separate problems. The latter question is one of finality not of the individuals but of the social system as a unity. Perhaps the most outstanding representative of this position is H. Janne. Janne is an exception to the general orientation of the Anglo-American functionalists. Janne holds that the notion of function itself implies an objective finality. Social phenomena are processes which can be viewed as if they were unfolding toward achievement of definite ends. He illustrates this with the example of education. Thus, educational institutions pursue ends of their own, students strive for still different personal aims, but when the process of formal education is terminated, young people are prepared for life in society to such an extent as if there were a central force systematically directing the activities of individuals and groups, balancing the different particular aims one against another for the sake of society.[7]

Much of the criticism of functionalism decries its teleological pretensions and yet admits that teleology is inherent in its holistic, self-regulatory or organismic view of society. Walter Buckley, for example, makes reference to Nagel's argument which tries to show that teleological explanation can be substituted by simple productively causal explanation. Yet, Buckley states that a certain degree of teleology is implied in functionalism in its appeal not to the purpose, but the end effect or 'final cause'[8] But even if this could be eradicated in the way suggested by Nagel, still there might be a place for teleology in the functional methodology on other accounts. Buckley makes reference to Radcliffe-Brown, whose normative concern with the problem of order and disorder in society has led him to view social phenomena as either leading to society's 'health' or else producing its disease. In either case explanation of the phenomena is in terms of their end effects.[9]

Similarly, Carl G. Hempel says that it is quite true that hypotheses of self-regulation, which are characteristic of functionalism, seem to have a teleological character, asserting, as they do, that 'within specified conditions systems of some particular kind will tend toward a state within the class R, which thus assumes the appearance of a final cause determining the behaviour of the system.' However, says Hempel,

> for most of the self-regulatory phenomena that come within the purview of functional analysis, the attribution of purposes is an illegitimate transfer of the concept of purpose from its domain of significant applicability to a much wider domain, where it is devoid of objective empirical import.[10]

Yet Hempel admits that perhaps it is precisely this psychological association of the concept of function with that of purpose that, although methodologically unwarranted, nevertheless accounts for the appeal and apparent plausibility of functional analysis as a mode of explanation.

One branch of criticism of teleology in functionalism asserts that the entire question is basically semantic since the teleological statements do not really say anything more than is stated by the logic of simple productively causal explanation. Accordingly, these critics say that all teleological statements in functionalism can be reformulated in a productively causal manner without loss in content. The most outstanding of these critics is Ernest Nagel. We will take up Nagel's argument in detail later on.

In summary, it can be stated that (1) on the whole, up to date very little has been said about teleology in functionalism by the functionalists themselves or by the critics of functionalism. In fact, most of the statements on teleology in functionalism are in the form of side remarks rather than substantive treatises. Nagel's treatment can be considered an exception, even though it is rather short. (2) There seems to be a kind of consensus among the functionalist writers and their critics that teleology is, all in all, an illegitimate method of explanation, at least as far as functionalism is concerned. (3) A substantive part of the criticism of the use of teleology in functionalism suggests that all the seemingly teleological statements in functionalism can be reformulated either in such a way as to offer explanation through motives of the participating individuals, or in such a way as to become simply productively causal explanations. Yet, (4) many outstanding functionalists, such as Parsons, Levy, and others, employ language which is apparently teleological and carries a telecausal explanatory import.

FORMULATION OF THE PRINCIPLE OF TELECAUSALITY

Meaning of the Principle

Telecausality means circumscription of the multiplicity of productive causes by their effects. It is a nexus in the future of the multiplicity of productive causes; an adaptation of the productive causes to the future. In other words, the principle expresses the idea of directed action and the idea of *means-ends:* the multiple productive causes are seen as differentiated means to an end implied in their common effect, and therefore in some way determined by it.[11]

The question of telecausality thus refers to the second aspect of the causal problem in functionalism, that of Ay causing x in the formula 'the function of x for y is A'.

Characteristics of Telecausality

1. *Repetition or multiplicity of coincidences.* This is not a phenomenon as such, but a repetition or concordance of phenomena.[12] Rather than a phenomenon, it is an intelligible realtion between phenomena. Thus:

$$\left\{ \begin{array}{l} \text{if } x, \text{then } y \\ \text{if } x, \text{then } y \\ \text{if } x, \text{then } y \end{array} \right\} \quad \text{then no } x \text{ without } y$$

Note that no necessity (uniqueness of bond, continuity of action) is implied between x and y, since the argument states only that y is preceded by x repetitively. It states that since x keeps reappearing as a productive cause of y, it can occur only if y is its effect. It does not say that x occurs because it is produced by y, but it says that x occurs because it keeps producing y. In that sense y determines x.

Rather than on necessity, the argument rests only on the impossibility of occurrence of x if it did not produce y. This impossibility is assessed from the repetition of x as a productive cause of y.

2. *Coincidence of different productive causalities.* Basically, this is the same argument as repetition: 'When a great number of phenomena, very different in every other point of view, yet present one common and constant circumstance, this circumstance may be given as the cause.'[13]
Thus:

$$\text{if} \begin{cases} \text{if } x, \text{ then } z \\ \text{if } k, \text{ then } l \\ \text{if } o, \text{ then } p \\ \text{if } n, \text{ then } .. \end{cases} \text{then } y; \text{ then} \begin{cases} \text{no } x \text{ producing } z \\ \text{no } k \text{ producing } l \\ \text{no } o \text{ producing } p \\ \text{no } n \ldots \end{cases} \text{without } y$$

if x, if k, if o, if $n \ldots$, then y; then no x, k, o, $n \ldots$ without y.

We set out, in short, from a fixed point which is given us by experience as an effect; but this effect only being possible by an incalculable mass of coincidences, it is this agreement between so many coincidences and a certain effect which constitutes precisely the proof of finality.

We see in this agreement the *criterion* which transforms the effect into an *end* and the causes into means.

Otherwise, the agreement appears without cause and purely arbitrary.[14]

Thus y appears as a cause in the same way as in the case of repetition.

3. *Relation of repetition or coincidence of different productive causalities to the future.*

The agreement of several phenomena, bound together with a future determinate phenomenon, supposes a cause in which that future phenomenon is ideally represented, and the probability of this presumption increases with the complexity of the concordant phenomena and the number of the relations which unite them to the final phenomena.[15]

The phenomena have not only a relation to the past (productive causality), but also a relation to the future and appear to us conditioned not only by their (productive) causes, but also by their effects.[16]

The effect already pre-exists in the cause producing it and hence directs and circumscribes its action.

This correlation to the future cannot be comprehended excepting that the future phenomenon already pre-exists in a certain fashion in the efficient (productive) cause and directs its actions.[17]

Therefore:

if x, if z, if k, if ... n, then y

In productive causality, if we were to explain x, z, k, ... n, we would have to resort to the antecedent conditions. Adequacy, invariability, uniqueness of bond, and continuity of action all refer to conditions before occurrence of the phenomenon: if x, then y—tries precisely to explain y in terms of x preceding it (antecedent to it). Thus to explain x, z, k, ... n, we would have to look for w, v, j, ... m, and our explanantion would be: if w, then x, if v, then z, if j, then k, if m, then n.

In telecausality x, z, k, ... n are explained in terms of their effect y. Hence we resort to a future condition. Our explanation is in terms: no x, z, k, ... n, without y which they produce. In this sense x, z, k, ... n appear as means to the end y. It must be re-emphasized that telecausality refers to multiplicity of productive causality and tries to explain its coincidence.

To sum up:

Finality is predetermination of the parts by the idea of the whole. The whole is not a simple effect, but also a cause, and the parts would not effect that arrangement if the whole had not beforehand commanded it.[18]

This implies self-regulation. The parts refer to the multiplicity of productive causality, the whole to the specific coincidence of this multiplicity. The specific coincidence hence is telecausality determining the multiple productive causality. The parts thus are means for the whole; it is the only way they can be explained as integrated or organized into a unit whole. 'The organized being is the being in which all is reciprocally end and means.'[19]

Telecausal explanation is explanation in terms of a self-regulating system, and vice versa, every self-regulating system implies telecausality.

TELECAUSAL CHARACTERISTICS IN FUNCTIONALISM

Repetition of Phenomena: Patterns of Behaviour

Patterns of behaviour constitute the starting point of functionalism. Functionalists have no quarrel about it and, in fact, today few sociologists, functionalists or otherwise, would disagree that this can be taken as a non-disputable axiom of all scientific sociology.[20] The first step of Merton's paradigm for functional analysis is recognition of 'standardized (i.e., patterned and repetitive)' items of behaviour.[21] There can be no functional analysis without it; that the object of analysis be standardized, says Merton, is the basic requirement of functionalism.

In functionalism, the meaning of the notion of patterns is tied up with that of the notion of structure. Sometimes the concept of structure is used interchangeably with that of patterns, but more often, structure is held to be made up of patterns, so that patterns are seen as units of structure.[22] Most functionalists would probably agree that structure

61

involves two ideas, that of arrangement of units and that of uniformity of units. The meaning of these ideas, however, is far from clear, especially because they permit interpretation in terms of different assumptions. First, is the arrangement and uniformity of units (i.e., patterns of action) an empirical reality, or is it only a mental construct forged to help us understand empirical reality? Secondly, does the concept of structure imply the notion of time or does it exclude it, i.e., is the arrangement of uniform elements an arrangement in time, that is, repetitiveness, or is it an arrangement in space? The second question is, of course, more relevant to our study, but it is contingent upon the first one.

The first question, however, has two further aspects. If structure is considered to be a construct, what type of a construct is it, is it an abstraction derived from concrete reality, or is it a heuristic model, imposed on empirical reality to enable us to understand it?

Claude Levi-Strauss has expounded the latter position. Social structure for him has nothing to do with empirical reality. It is a model and must be distinguished from the concept of social relations. Social relations consist of the raw materials out of which the models making up social structure are built. They make up the concrete empirical reality in any given society; social structure remains only a method to be applied to any concrete social reality for the purposes of analysis.[23]

Both Marion Levy, Jr. and S. F. Nadel would not go as far as Levi-Strauss. For them social structure remains grounded in empirical reality. Thus says Levy:

> The term *structure* as used here means a pattern, i.e., an observable uniformity, of action or operation. The general form of this concept is deliberately left in to cover a wide range of possibilities from highly stable uniformities to highly fleeting ones. . . . Any event may contain an element indicative of a structure insofar as it is considered with regard to its non-unique aspects or characteristics.[24]

Structure, however, remains for Levy an abstract concept. The patterns of action, says Levy, do not exist concretely as patterns. They are not concrete objects in the same sense as sticks and stones are. They 'exist' and are 'empirically verifiable' in the same sense that the squareness of a box exists and is empirically verifiable. In short, structure is an abstraction, but an abstraction derived from empirically observed reality, or more precisely, it is an inference from the concrete actions of concrete individuals or groups of individuals. What can be observed are the uniformities of action of the same or different individuals, what is inferred is the unitary character of all these uniformities, their existence as part of the whole.[25]

A similar position is taken by S. F. Nadel. Nadel's treatment of social structure is perhaps the most complete yet. Nadel takes issue with Levi-Strauss's, as well as Leach's, view of social structure as a model. For Levi-Strauss and Leach, says Nadel, structure is purely an explanatory construct meant to provide the key to the observed social reality, to explain the logic behind social reality and thus to improve on it. For Nadel, social structure still is social reality itself or an aspect of it and not the logic behind it. True, it has a remoteness from the real condition, but this remoteness goes with progressive abstraction.[26] Structural analysis, however sophisticated, ultimately remains no more than a descriptive method and not a piece of explanation. If social structure is to be considered as a model at all, it will have to be a statistical model, since unlike other models, a statistical model does not offer any explanatory laws, but simply a numerical, descriptive picture of the social situation.[27]

Therefore, in one sense structure is a property of empirical data; it is something they exhibit inasmuch as we can observe an ordered arrangement of parts. It remains an abstraction, however, inasmuch as the concept ignores all that is not order or arrangement, but which also characterizes the same empirical data.[28]

Talcott Parsons' view of social structure does not differ basically from either Nadel's or Levy's. However, he considers structure in the context of the social system, and views 'structure' as a property of the latter. Thus, a social system has a structure inasmuch as it can be said to contain differentiated, segmented and specified, yet stable, patterns. But differentiation of functions, segmentation of subunits and specification of norms is an empirical problem. Social structure therefore is to be studied through empirical investigation, but it is ultimately explained by a model of a self-regulating system. Viewing structure as a property of the social system is a combination of both empirical investigation and explanation through a model.[29] We will return to this problem later. Here it suffices to say that when it comes to actual research, viewing social structure as an explanatory model is not a fruitful methodology for, as Nadel points out, it becomes impossible to even speak of studying social structure; you do not study or investigate a model—you build it on the basis of empirical investigations, and the building process, culminating in logical deduction, makes possible better understanding of the original empirical phenomena.[30]

In regard to telecausality, if the patterns of behaviour which are represented in the concept of social structure are not the phenomena to be explained, but being part of a model are the means of explaining, then there is no case for telecausality, since there are no patterned phenomena to be explained. The functionalism of Merton, Parsons, Levy and many others, however, considers patterns as given phenomena to be explained as the end of functional analysis.[31]

If the concept of structure refers to an aspect of empirical phenomena, does it nevertheless imply time or is it divorced from it? Marion Levy takes the latter position. According to him, inasmuch as structure is an abstraction, it is also an abstraction from time. Structure remains a static picture of uniformity and arrangement of positions.[32] Not so for Nadel. One reason that we do ascribe 'structure' to phenomena, says Nadel, is their succession in time, "an interrelation of parts defined by the criteria of 'earlier' and 'later', as in a sentence or pieces of music."[33] We speak only *as if* the positions were fixed in structure, but it is only as if, and if our descriptive structural categories do not explicitly refer to the time element, we yet imply it. Nadel states that the terms 'invariance,' 'continuity' or 'constancy' involved in the notion of structure refer, in fact, to recurrence and repetitiveness, and therefore social structure must be visualized as a sum of processes in time.[34] Trying to explain how social structure is both an abstraction and yet implies time, Nadel, in a very instructive passage, states:

> Our hypotheses and as-if constructions are not fantasies but well grounded, both methodologically and empirically. For the empirical constancies do exist and are observable. . . . Let us admit this, however. The constancies which we, the anthropologists in the field, actually observe are of short range. We do see repetitions, regularities, the reproduction of roles and relationships, and the restoring of (small-scale) disturbed states —as in disputes, quarrels, unexpected fatalities, etc. But we also assume them to last longer than the period of observation. In other words, we anticipate the appropriate scale of macrotime on which our assumptions would really be proved. We surely have good grounds for doing so: they lie in the observable maintenance machineries; in past continuities, ascertainable with a fair degree of reliability; and last but not least, in our general faith that a living society will not change its shape as soon as our backs are turned. . . . (It) would not change for that reason, which is the crux of our faith and the foundation of our whole science. . . .
> But if no workable constancies emerge (after a larger-scale change or disturbance of society), then there is no society for us to study and no structure to define; for the assumptions or postulates underlying our methods also prescribe the nature of the data that can be studied by them.[35]

It is this anticipation of macro-time that, in effect, makes us use static concepts when referring to repetitive constancies, but the meaning of regular repetition is not lost, just as we say of two seaports that 'they *are* linked by boat,' —meaning that boats move between them more or less regularly.[36] A better analogy would be the analysis in physics of atomic or molecular structures, where the analysis is of movements in time, but the regularities of these movements can be represented in a more static manner by 'orbits'. Hence, the time dimension is not only implicit in the concept of structure, but actually constitutes a condition of it.[37] It is ultimately repetitive behaviour which constitutes the starting point of structural analysis and functional theory construction.[38]

Coincidence of Phenomena: Equilibrium as an Empirical Generalization

The kind of phenomena that functional analysis is called upon to explain is thus typically some repetitive, recurrent behaviour of groupings of people. This, however, is only part of the story. As was said previously, patterns of behaviour are the object of explanation of any scientific approach in sociology, functionalist or not. Functionalism goes further. Empirically existing patterns of behaviour might be the starting point for functionalism, but what empirically manifests itself is also coexistence with the institutionalized structural patterns of conflicting pattern tendencies, tendencies toward deviance, tendencies toward disintegration and change. Yet, it can be observed that in these tendencies the structural patterns remain constant over periods of time. The stability or order of the social system is therefore not just a matter of institutionalized patterns, but a matter of both the institutionalized patterns and the conflicting pattern tendencies. In this sense the stability of the social system, to the extent that it can be empirically assessed, is a coincidence to be explained. This then becomes the central problem of functionalism. To quote Parsons:

> (The) elements of the constancy of pattern must constitute a fundamental point of reference for the analysis of process in the

(social) system. From a certain point of view these processes are to be defined as the processes of maintenance of the constant patterns. But of course these are empirical constancies, so we do not assume any inherent reason why they have to be maintained. It is simply a fact that, as described in terms of a given frame of reference, these constancies are often found to exist, and theory can thus be focused on the problems presented by their existence. They may cease to exist, by the dissolution of the distinctive boundary-maintaining system and its assimilation to the environment, or by transformation into other patterns. But the fact that they do exist, at given times and places, still serves as the theoretical focus for analysis.[39]

There is a further aspect to this question of social equilibrium. According to Parsons, the social system, or in this case society itself, consists of 'loosely federated congeries' of systems and subsystems of different types, each operating in its own right, with its own normative patterns and equilibrium problems.[40] Parsons assumes that there is always the danger that component units will slip out of field and operate on their own without relevance to the common condition. As Devereaux puts it, 'that any sort of equilibrium is achieved at all, as it evidently is in most societies most of the time, represents for Parsons something both of miracle and challenge'.[41]

It is essential to have a clear meaning of the concept of equilibrium. The concept has been used, though often uncritically, in at least two senses: as an empirical generalization and as a theoretical proposition. As an empirical generalization, it describes basically the series of events which results in a balance of counteracting forces (action tendencies). This is the meaning of equilibrium as explained above—the observable equilibrium, in Parsons' terms, a process by which a system can be observed either to come to terms with the external or internal exigencies, without essential change in its own structure, or otherwise fail to come to terms and undergo other processes such as structural change.[42]

As a theoretical proposition, however, the concept includes the assumption of a self-regulating system. Self-regulation means negative feed-back, i.e., ability to generate forces which restore the displaced equilibrium. A self-regulating system, hence, includes devices for a negative feed-back.[43] An example of such a device are tariffs which prevent price fluctuations from going below certain limits whenever large quantities of foreign low priced goods are imported. A negative feed-back device is usually seen as a sort of thermostat which increases or reduces the heat throttle according to whether its thermometer registers above or below a set value.[44]

The distinction between equilibrium as an empirical generalization and as a theoretical proposition must, therefore, be clearly understood. The first use of the concept is descriptive, the second is explanatory. Confusion of the two meanings can lead only to unnecessary misunderstanding as, for example, in the case of Walter Buckley. Buckley accuses functionalism of tautological reasoning on the grounds that functional statements are always *ex post facto* statements. Accordingly, functional explanation of why society functions says nothing more than is implied in the description of society. Functionalism explains reality by simply assessing what it is. Thus a basic principle of functional explanation is explanation through the social system prerequisites, such as provision for sexual recruitment, role differentiation, role assignment, communication, a shared articulated set of goals, normative regulation of means, socialization, etc. But all these prerequisites, argues Buckley, make up the definition of society in the first place, inasmuch as all societies which maintain themselves in existence include all these as their structural items. Hence, in effect, we are explaining the functioning of societies by simply describing how societies function.[45]

By this conclusion, however, Buckley confuses theory with fact, for what can be determined by observation is not society, or any social system, in the unitary sense of the word, but a coincidence of different phenomena. Definition of society is an interpretation of the observed empirical phenomena and not the phenomena themselves.

For Parsons, the coexistence of counteracting social forces is precisely the situation to be explained. His explanans is a theoretical model of self-regulative systems with devices for a negative feed-back. Nadel makes this methodology quite clear when he says:

> When making judgments on constancies, stability or equilibrium two considerations always enter. The first is a strictly empirical one, since, 'it is simply a fact that . . . these constancies are often found to exist'. The second is a heuristic one, the stipulated stability being a theoretical condition, a useful 'methodological fiction', required by the type of analysis we are after. It may in fact have the character of a postulate without which our particular investigation could not be carried out. Thus, if we are concerned (as in fact we are) with discovering the mutual determination of a plurality of elements, as in a 'system', we shall naturally assume, to begin with, that such a determination exists.[46]

It should be mentioned here at the outset that the principle of equilibrium as a heuristic device does not have to be understood necessarily in the Kantian sense, as a category of the mind. Its meaning is more that of an assumption which is not empirically proven but not empirically irrelevant.

RELATION TO THE FUTURE:
MODEL OF A SELF-REGULATING SYSTEM
AS EXPLANATORY DEVICE

The procedure of relating patterns of different productively causal phenomena to one effect which they are to produce in the future is the procedure of system construction. In this way the patterns of different independent productively causal phenomena become parts of a whole. Only through this relation to the future phenomenon can these different patterns be seen as a network rather than coincidence, as interdependent rather than independent.[47] Thus the parts are explainable in terms of the whole; they become means to an end and are therefore determined by it. The principle of equilibrium, therefore, is the principle of determinacy. As Nadel says:

> It is worth noting that, when we make these assumptions, in regard to societies or any other universe of discourse, it is not the equilibrium conditions *as such* which matter to us most or primarily. There is nothing inherently important about them. . . . The assumption of equilibrium is important only in a derived sense, as the logical consequence of that more fundamental assumption, that it makes sense to look for determinacy. If we believed in a social universe entirely characterized by the free will of all its elements, we should not need equilibrium assumptions; nor indeed could we use them in any profitable way.[48]

The functionalist assumption of a self-persistent, self-regulating system can be thus considered as an attempt to explain the empirically observed social equilibrium. That is, (a) the different social forces (action tendency patterns) are viewed as parts of a more or less integrated whole, and are explained in relation to this integration, as more or less contributing to it; (b) the system as a whole, through its mechanisms, influences and controls the social forces by inhibiting their disintegrative potentialities and stimulating their integrative potentialities. Hence, (c) implied is a schema of means and ends. Social forces, as action patterns, are seen as means for relative integration of the system, and the integration of the system is an end of action of the forces, and therefore explains their persistence. It remains to be shown how functionalism uses a means-ends schema of explanation. Before doing this, however, two things must be noted. First, there is a difference of views among the functionalists as to the significance of the system model, in particular the difference of views between Merton and Parsons. Secondly, there is a divergence of views as to the meaning of the notion of function. Both of these issues will be discussed respectively.

As Alvin Gouldner put it, Parsons' position can be regarded as a total commitment to the system model, while Merton's position has to be seen as a strategy of minimal commitment.[49] The reasons for this divergence are several. It will be useful to summarize Gouldner's argument on two significant points of this divergence. For one thing, there is a difference in focus of analysis between the two men. Parsons' central problem is the social system as such,—in particular, the question of how and why it is maintained as a going concern. Empirically identifiable units are important primarily as they enter into the maintenance of the system in the satisfaction of its needs. In contrast, Merton does not require that the problematic unit be related to any postulated need of the system. His focus is on the empirically identifiable unit of behaviour itself, with a view simply to account for its consequences for the environing social structures.[50]

More important between Parsons and Merton, however, are their differing views of theory construction in sociology. Parsons assumes that the *a priori* postulate of the social system requires also an *a priori* identification of the system's constituent parts and relationships among them. In this way the total anatomy of the social system is to be conceptually constituted prior to the empirical investigation of concrete behaviour patterns. This for Merton is begging the question. For whether or not a given anatomical element of the social system should be postulated is resolvable only by empirical research. Unlike Parsons, Merton tends to emphasize that empirical operations are necessarily involved in the very admission of elements as parts of the social system. This seems to be the meaning of his 'middle range' approach.[51]

However, the difference between Parsons and Merton seems to lie even deeper—specifically, in the meaning of the concept of function. As noted above, the functionalist assumption of a self-persistent, self-regulating system is an attempt to explain the empirically observed social equilibrium. But the relation of the components of the empirically observed social equilibrium to the self-regulating system model is accomplished through the use of the concept of function. The concept of function, because of its moot meaning, has been perhaps the most confused concept in functionalism. I suggest that the lack of clarity about this concept derives from the failure or perhaps unwillingness of the functionalist writers to admit telecausality as part of the method of their analysis.

THE CONCEPT OF FUNCTION: ITS SIGNIFICANCE IN THE SOCIAL SYSTEM MODEL

The concept of function has been used in quite a variety of meanings. Raymond Firth and Robert Merton have tried to list a number of such usages. Those most common in scholarly literature have been summarized in four categories; function in the sense of activity or task-performance of an object or entity; function in the sense of relation of interdependence with activities of other entities; function in the sense of interdependence of special quality, especially in regard to ends, such as maintenance of a system; and function in the sense of consequences of structures or structural items.[52]

The first meaning of the word is the least technical. Yet it is often used by sociologists, at times interchangeably with other meanings. Parsons himself has used the word in this sense. This is actually the popular meaning of the word and hence is most readily understood by the sociologically unsophisticated reader.

The second meaning, that of interdependence, is allied to the mathematical concept of function, designating a quantity variable in relation to other quantities in terms of which it may be expressed or on which its value depends. The meaning here is that of covariance, a relation which is reversible in terms of cause and effect.[53] This meaning of the notion never had much use in either sociology or social anthropology. An interesting exception in sociology is Homans' much criticized attempt to study human inter-action simply in terms of the degree of interdependence.[54]

The third sense of the term—function as an orientation toward given ends, has been much more widespread and theoretically fruitful, both in sociology and social anthro-pology. We shall return to this notion presently, after discussing the Mertonian definition of function, function in the fourth sense of the term—as a consequence or an aggregate of consequences.

CRITIQUE OF MERTON'S DEFINITION OF THE CONCEPT OF FUNCTION

Merton's use of the concept of function involves two basic elements, that of 'multiple consequences' and that of a 'net balance of an aggregate of consequences'. In defining func-tions as multiple consequences, Merton carefully dis-tinguishes between the notion of function and that of aim, motive or purpose. The latter are subjective dispositions. The former refers to consequences which are 'observable' and 'objective'. These can be either positive or negative. Thus, '*functions* are those observed consequences which make for the adaptation or adjustment of a given system; and *dysfunctions*, those observed consequences which lessen the adaptation or adjustment of the system.'[55] In short, the notion of function is understood by Merton as the observ-able objective consequences for the state of the system.

Unfortunately, Merton does not make clear what he exactly means by the term consequence. From his discussion of the entire issue it seems most logical to conclude that his meaning of the term is that of the effect of productive causality, not necessarily a direct effect, but certainly at least an intercausal effect in the sense discussed above. No more seems to be implied. There is no idea of means-ends, nor of consequences having any determinacy over the functioning structural items. It might be argued, however, to the contrary, that Merton allows the notion of function a determinacy of the persistence of the structural patterns by the need they fulfil. Thus at one point of his analysis of the functioning of the political machine Merton says:

> The functional deficiencies of the official structure generate an alternative (unofficial) structure to fulfil existing needs somewhat more effectively (italics omitted). Whatever its specific historical origins, the political machine persists as an apparatus for satisfying otherwise unfilled needs of diverse groups in the population.[65]

It appears, then, that Merton, in addition to productive causality, implies some telecausality in his notion of function. However, Merton is ambiguous on this point. His use of the word 'needs' is deceptive. He uses it interchangeably with the word 'function' itself. In fact, although in the beginning of his essay on 'Manifest and Latent Functions' he uses the word need a number of times, towards the end of the essay he completely substitutes for it the word function. Instead of saying, as in the passage quoted above, that the political machine fulfils some needs of the diverse subgroups, towards the end of the essay he repeatedly states that if fulfils some functions for these diverse subgroups. If one were to substitute here for the term 'functions' Merton's overt definition of functions as consequences, then the entire formulation would make little sense. This, however, does not reflect simply a careless use of terms. Merton's ambiguity in the use of the term function has a deeper source. Though in actual analysis Merton has difficulty in finding a substitute for the notion of 'needs', overtly he has criticized the use of the notion in functional analysis on the grounds that it is tautological or *ex post facto* and hence does not explain anything more than is implied in the actual identification of the functioning structural item. This argument is similar to that of Buckley. Hence, an adequate description of what the political machine does as an economic unit will also involve a statement of its functions, i.e., the consequences it has for the diverse sub-groups. It is thus as an effect of productive causality that Merton's use of the term function must be understood.[57]

By the same token, Merton's '*net balance* of an aggregate of consequences' must be understood as a coincidence of effects of productive causality. This coincidence might be either an integration or disintegration of the social system. In either case, the ultimate state of the social system is an accidental situation, a lucky or unlucky coincidence of consequences. Perhaps Merton would not like to go that far, but it is the only way his functionalism can be understood if one is to take his overt definition of the notion of function seriously.

The Mertonian concept of function does not imply any idea of a self-regulating system. There is no reference in it to the idea that the effects of productive causality are in any way system-oriented, i.e., that they are means to an end. As was pointed out above, Merton considers the idea of a self-regulating system not as a workable assumption, but as something to be proven by empirical research.[58] In effect, what Merton has done by his application to functionalism of the concepts of consequences and net balance of consequences has been to transfer notions borrowed from a model used in mechanics to a theory which uses a model borrowed from biology. The two remain incongruous.

Most functionalists, however, do not conceive of 'function' in this Mertonian way. The prevalent meaning of the term implies the idea of orientation towards satisfaction of needs. The structural elements do not simply contribute to the integration or disintegration of the total system, they do so via satisfaction or lack of satisfaction of specific extant needs. Hence, the relationship between the structural elements and the given state of the system is not simply one of productive intercausality. Ralph Linton says that every element of culture, simply because it is shared, can be said to have the function of contributing to social integration. However, he continues, such universal ascription of function is the *reductio ad absurdum* of the whole idea. If function is to have any meaning for the study of culture (or we can say any social system), the concept must be made more specific. Elements which are without utility may still have function and meaning, if, in themselves they provide responses to particular needs of the individual or group. Thus the inclusion of medical rituals in many occupational complexes does not contribute directly to the success of the work but does contribute towards the assurance and peace of mind of the worker.[59]

Consequently, Linton defines function as the contribution which any particular element of culture makes towards the satisfaction of a particular need or needs. On the other hand, if an element meets no needs at all, even if it is accepted as part of the total shared culture, it nevertheless must be said to be functionless. Being part of the total culture, it can be said to contribute to its integration. But to say that this is its function is meaningless, unless it can be shown that it fulfils some needs whose satisfaction reflects itself in the total state of the culture. Linton is free of any panfunctionalism, i.e., he does not assume that any cultural element must have some function simply because it exists as part of culture. In this Linton diverges from Malinowski. But otherwise Malinowski's notion of function is the same as Linton's.[60] Both Linton and Malinowski, however, differ from such functionalists as Parsons, Radcliffe-Brown, and Levy in one important respect. The needs which they emphasize are not formulated so much as culture's needs but are discussed more as needs of the individuals, so that the culture's functioning appears to be explainable in terms of the individual and his needs, be they biological or derived. Perhaps a reason for this is that both of them are dealing with culture rather than social organization or society, and culture does not represent a concrete system in the same sense as either society or personality does.

Talcott Parsons and Marion J. Levy, Jr. define functions also as contributions which structural elements make towards satisfaction of given needs, but the given needs are those of the social system as such. In this manner the social system is assumed to be self-regulative.

Parsons originally used the term 'function' without much scrutiny. He used it often in the sense of task-performance. The functional problems of the social system were simply those of smooth working of the system.[61] In the *Social System*, the functional problems are more consciously defined as those of fulfilment of the system's needs. Thus, one of the basic functional problems of the social system is conceived by Parsons to be allocation of roles; Parsons says:

> Roles are, from the point of view of the functioning of the social system, the primary mechanisms through which the essential functional prerequisites of the system are met. There is the same order of relationship between roles and functions relative to the system in social systems, as there is between organs and functions in the organism.[62]

With Parsons' most recent reformulation of the notion of the system prerequisites, the idea of function becomes even more specifically interlocked with the problem of the system's need-satisfaction. According to it, the functioning of the system as a whole is to be understood through the functioning of the system's subsystems. But the functioning of the subsystems themselves is the process of fulfilling the needs or prerequisites of the total system. Hence the notion of the function is made practically synonymous with the process of system need-satisfaction.[63] The next chapter will examine Parsons' notion of the needs of the social system and his theory of the social need-satisfaction process in detail. Here it should be added that Marion Levy, perhaps the foremost commentator on Parsons, goes even one step further. According to him, function refers to the operation of the system through time. In no way is it just a consequence of the operation of the system, as Merton would have it, but an integral part of that operation itself.[64]

In summary, the prevalent meaning of the concept of

function is the meaning of orientation of the social system's structural elements towards satisfaction of given needs of the system. These needs, therefore, must be seen as ends and the elements, i.e., structural items or their properties, as means for fulfilment of these needs. The social system can be said to be in a state of equilibrium, i.e., relatively integrated, if these ends are relatively met. The relative integration implies that there are elements which do not fulfil the needs, or that there are means not 'adequately' related to the ends.

CRITIQUE OF MERTON'S DISTINCTION BETWEEN THE MANIFEST AND LATENT FUNCTIONS

Since it was first formulated in 1948, Merton's distinction between manifest and latent functions has acquired among sociologists a rather widespread usage. The distinction highlights the methodology of a number of foremost sociologists and anthropologists of the recent and not so recent past, and Merton's explicit formulation of it has ever since held a promise of fruitful sociological inquiry and research.

It is surprising, however, that until today no systematic evaluation of the distinction has been undertaken, even though informally many sociologists will admit that the distinction remains problematic. Academic rumours have it that Merton himself has modified his original formulation in his university lectures; nothing, however, has appeared in print.

The trouble with the distinction is that it confuses the issue of intention with that of recognition. Marion Levy has recognized the confusion in his *Structure of Society*, but refused to elaborate his evaluation of it on the grounds that such elaboration is futile unless reference is made to specific empirical analysis.[65] There are, however, two sides to the issue. No doubt empirical research is necessary for refining sociological concepts, but, on the other hand, as much as possible theoretical concepts should be made clear on the theoretical level itself, especially if it concerns the meaning of a major theoretical distinction, as certainly the manifest-latent functions distinction is.

For Merton, manifest functions are consequences both intended and recognized by the participants in the system, latent functions are consequences which are neither intended nor recognized.[66] Intention and recognition, however, are two different things. It is possible to intend an effect but not recognize it, or not to intend it, but recognize it. In the latter case the effect would not derive from the particular intention. In the first case the intention itself might be either conscious or subconscious. Accordingly, the following modification of the Mertonian distinction of functions can be devised.

First, Merton's distinction between manifest and latent functions more properly should be a distinction between intended and unintended consequences or effects. Secondly, the intended effects can be subdivided into those consciously intended and those subconsciously or unconsciously intended. For the sake of retaining Merton's terminology, the former can be called, at least for the present, the 'manifested functions' and the latter 'unmanifested functions'. The term 'latent functions' can remain to identify the unintended effects. Thirdly, all of these, the manifested, the unmanifested and the latent functions can be divided into effects which are either recognized by the participants in the system or unrecognized by them. All this can be summarized as follows:

Manifested functions = consciously intended effects.
1. Recognized; when the participants are aware of the effects taking place.
2. Unrecognized; when the participants are not aware of the effects taking place.[67]

Unmanifested functions = subconsciously intended effects.
1. Recognized; when the participants are aware of the effects

taking place, even though they are not aware that they have intended them.

2. Unrecognized; when the participants are neither aware of the effects taking place nor of their intention of these effects.

Latent functions = unintended effects, either consciously or unconciously. Effects which follow as a result of intending something else.

1. Recognized; when the participants are aware of the effects.

2. Unrecognized; when the participants are not aware of the effects.

Introduction of the variable of subconscious intention into the schema is necessary because it is important to distinguish between intention of an effect and recognition of it. The basic point at issue is that recognition of an effect does not mean, as Merton would have it, coming to intend it. That is, latent functions, as meaning unintended effects, when recognized, do not become 'manifest' functions, even in the Mertonian sense of the word 'manifest'. Unfortunately the contrary of this has been often assumed.[68]

The functionalist's interest is primarily in the latent functions.[69] The manifested and the unmanifested functions are of interest only inasmuch as they are in a dynamic relationship with the latent functions. But this relationship is much different from that existing between the manifested and the unmanifested functions.

The crux of this dynamic relationship between the intended (manifested or unmanifested) and the unintended (latent) consequences is a matter of what follows for the social system on account of the fact that the participants intend something else. If the participants were to intend the unintended consequences (previously unintended), then these consequences, most probably, would not be effected at all. For example, on the psychological level: If prayer effects peace of mind, it is because the praying person intends something else, i.e., effective communication with the addressee of the prayer. If the worshipper were to intend peace of mind, using prayer as means, peace of mind would not ensue. The psychologists tell us that it ensues precisely because the worshipper is able to take his mind off the problem of his peace of mind.

An example on the sociological level: If persons pursue their private profit-interests and what follows is a capitalistic social integration, if they were to intend this integration rather than private profit-interest in their action, such capitalistic social integration would not be effected. As economists and sociologists tell us, individualistic values rather than collectivistically oriented values are responsible for the capitalist system.

Awareness of everything that happens as a result of one's pursuit of his intentions does not mean intention of these results. We might be quite aware that religion is related to social solidarity, but this does not mean that our awareness makes us pursue religion for the sake of social solidarity. Awareness or lack of awareness of the unintended effects is not in itself significant.

The unintended effects can be seen as (1) simple effects of productive causality (Merton's notion), or (2) as related to a determining principle outside of the productive causes, in terms of which the productive causes themselves are seen as effects of telecausality, i.e., means to an end. As explained above, functionalism emphasizes the latter. The unintended effects are therefore *processes* taking place within the social system, *regardless* of whether the participants are aware of them or not. What Merton calls unintended consequences, in the telecausal context has a more precise meaning as processes of the social system. It is understood that the processes are not those intended by the participants. This is implied in the notion of self-persistence and self-regulation of the social system. However, these processes can be discovered and fruitfully studied only in reference to what is intended by the participants. The two are interdependent. Even though the latter is explained telecausally as means of the former, the former is understood to be productively caused by the latter. The dynamic relationship between the two is a fruitful field for research, and it seems that gradually more research is being done in this area.[70] But for functionalism the *explanans* always remains (at least as long as the assumption of a self-regulating system is not changed) the social process, albeit unintended, rather than the intended social behaviour.

Chapter IV

TALCOTT PARSONS'
MEANS-ENDS SCHEMA OF
FUNCTIONAL EXPLANATION

Following the stages of development of his own thought, Parsons' theory concerns two basic levels, that of the ego-alter role behaviour (microfunctionalism), and that of the social system in general (macrofunctionalism). The basic logic of explanation, however, is the same on both levels; it follows the formula that what is the end of action for one subject of interaction (actor or a social subsystem), is the means for fulfilling an end of another subject of interaction (another actor or another social subsystem), and vice versa. This type of interaction is seen by Parsons as the basic process of integration of the social system.

EGO-ALTER INTERACTION ANALYSIS:
PARSONS' MICROFUNCTIONALISM

A fundamental starting point for Parsons' early sociology is the notion of 'complementarity of expectations' and the notion of 'double contingency'. Accordingly, between any two social actors, the action of each is oriented to the expectations of the other. Expectations of an ego always imply the expectations of one or more alters. When patterned, the expectations, together with sanctions attached to them, make up social roles.
Thus,

what an actor is expected to do in a given situation both by

83

himself and by others constitutes the expectations of that role. What the relevant alters are expected to do, contingent on ego's action, constitutes the sanctions (both in the positive and the negative sense). Role expectations and sanctions are therefore, in terms of the content of action, the *reciprocal of each other*. What are sanctions to ego are also role-expectations to alter, and vice versa.[1]

Inherent in this complementarity of expectations is also a double contingency of ego-alter need-satisfaction. That is, satisfaction of ego's needs or fulfilment of his goals becomes dependent on alter's willingness to do what is expected of him, and vice versa. Conformity with ego's expectations on alter's part is a condition of ego's goal realization. Conformity with alter's expectations is thus ego's means of achieving alter's conformity with ego's expectations. Ideally, a 'well' established system of interaction is such in which conformity with expectations becomes a need-disposition in itself. When this happens, then alter's fulfilling of ego's role-expectations reinforces ego's need-disposition to fulfil alter's role-expectations. Parsons summarizes the entire argument in this manner:

> An established state of a social system is a process of complementary interaction of two or more individual actors in which each conforms with the expectation of the other('s) in such a way that alter's reactions to ego's actions are positive sanctions which serve to reinforce his given need-dispositions and thus to fulfil his given expectations. This stabilized or equilibrated interaction process is the fundamental point of reference for all dynamic motivational analysis of social process.[2]

Parsons goes on to make a very significant assumption. He says that the tendency to maintain the interaction between the actors, once the complementarity of role-expectations is established, can be considered non-problematical, and can be assumed as the 'first law of social process'. That is, this tendency does not require any explanation, since the explanation for it is contained in its own nature. In other words, once the motivation to maintain interaction has been established, the interaction will maintain itself in a stable manner. This is significant in view of the assumption of self-regulation of social systems. Negative feed-back is possible only if actors are oriented to maintain their system of interaction. The effects of the means-ends nature of the ego-alter interaction is to create mutual sanctioning which will counter any deviation on the part of either the ego or the alter. Any such deviation sets in motion forces which function to restore the *status quo*. It is therefore possible to talk in any realistic manner about the social system regulating itself or acting in its own right to preserve its integration only inasmuch as the actors participating in it are motivated to maintain the *status quo* of their interaction.

By the same token, any tendency toward deviation from a stable interaction system is a question of motivational failure. Motivation to fulfil role-expectations is not automatic. It must be both established and continuously maintained. Specific mechanisms are therefore required to accomplish this. Parsons distinguishes two types of such mechanisms: socialization, a mechanism of establishing the motivation for fulfilment of role-expectations, and social control, a mechanism through which motivation for fulfilment of role-expectations is maintained.

The process of socialization highlights the commonly assessed fact that motivation to fulfil expected obligations is not inborn but has to be acquired through learning. To put it in other words, if an interaction between individuals is to be established and maintained in any stable manner, each individual cannot just do what he wants, but must learn what to want first. Before he has learned this, he will tend to act in ways which would upset the equilibrium of the interaction. Socialization is thus a learning process, but it is not learning in general, but a particular type of learning, one relevant to the establishment and maintenance of interaction between people. Five specific mechanisms through which such learning takes place are distinguished.

They are: reinforcement-extinction, inhibition, substitution, imitation and identification.[3]

Socialization, however, is not enough. The mechanism of social control is necessary because socialization itself is unable to counteract all the tendencies to deviance. Tendencies to deviance are motivations to depart from conformity with the normative standards shared by the interacting individuals. Hence tendencies to deviance are disruptive of the complementarity aspect of role behaviour. They represent failures to maintain the motivation for fulfilment of role-expectations. If tolerated beyond certain limits, they would tend to change or disintegrate the system of interaction. Therefore mechanisms are needed to counteract these tendencies—mechanisms which would discourage non-conformity and encourage conformity in order to maintain the established interaction. The mechanism of social control is then a motivational process which counteracts the motivations to deviance from fulfilment of role-expectations. It is thus a re-equilibrating process, i.e., it must always be stated relative to a 'given state of equilibrium of the system or sub-system which include specification of the normative patterns institutionalized in that sub-system, and the balance of motivational forces relative to conformity with and deviance from these patterns.'[4]

Parsons uses the terms 'process' and 'mechanism' in a rather confusing manner. For example, he says that the process of socialization takes place through mechanisms of learning, but the mechanisms of social control are, in effect, motivational processes.[5] The use of the terms here is uncritical. But this confusion of terminology will be less unforgiveable if we understand Parsons' objective in using either of these terms. The fundamental point of reference for Parsons' analysis of both socialization and social control is the equilibrium state of the social system, in this case the equilibrium state of role interaction system.[6] His concern is with the means which make role interaction possible. We can say that socialization is nothing but the function that learning and its components have for the social system; so also social control is the function which such things as division of labour, statutes of law, etc. perform for the system.

It is noteworthy, however, that Parsons rarely uses the terms function and consequence. He would rather talk about processes and mechanisms. Actually, Parsons seems to give more weight to the term process than to the term mechanism. He would rather define the latter in terms of the former, than the other way around. In view of his objectives, the term process seems to be more meaningful if understood as continuity of action fulfilling or failing to fulfil the needs of the system in which it occurs. Since maintenance of equilibrium is Parsons' crucial point of reference, continuity of action is an essential idea in his entire scheme. Defined in this manner, the concept of process expresses the notion that action is end-oriented, or is a means. Looked at from another point of view, process means the system in action, and therefore satisfaction of the system's needs is the means of keeping up, in continuity, the action of its structural components.

To avoid the pitfalls implied in the notion of function, especially to avoid defining it in terms of effects of productive causality, I suggest that the term be dropped from the functionalist vocabulary altogether. Instead, the term process should be used systematically.[7] Instead of saying that the family performs the function of motivating the prospective members of society to role-orientation, we should say that the family training of children is a process of reinforcing the role-orientation need. Or, to use Merton's example, instead of saying that the political machine in the U.S. functions to support, among other things, illegitimate business, we should say that the political behaviour in the U.S. is a process through which, among other things, (some) needs of illegitimate business are satisfied. Or, instead of saying that indirect, impersonal system of communication between the waitresses and the countermen in the restaurant system functions to maintain the system in a working condition through satisfaction of the countermen's status needs, we should say that indirect, impersonal communication between the two within the specific setting is a process through which the status needs of the countermen are satisfied, these needs being essential to the system.

The advantages that the use of the term process seems to have over the term function are several. First of all, it can produce greater precision, inasmuch as the functional argument becomes free from the varied connotations of the term function, especially the connotation that a specific function is *the* basic reason for a state of the social system. Secondly, the use of the term process accentuates much more than the term function the idea that the phenomenon under study is part of a whole. Since the term is borrowed from the biological sciences, it has the connotation of action of an organism, or action within an organism. Furthermore, the word process, by signifying persistence of movement, implies more definitively both the notion of continuity of action and the idea of institutionalization. The former is necessary in functionalism in view of its equilibrium assumption. The latter is the starting point for functional analysis, since its concern is with persistent patterns of behaviour.[8] Finally, the term process preserves the idea of telecausality, but frees it from the connotation of planned purpose. Process is a means of a certain effect, but the means is not necessarily an instrument of a planned design, but rather a means of functioning of a given body, regardless of any planning. This, in turn, accentuates the distinction which we have made between the intended (manifested or unmanifested) and the latent functions. Thus, it is suggested here that the use of the term process in place of the term function will help to make functional analysis more precise, more systematic and more fruitful in knowledge.

To sum up, Parsons' ego-alter interaction analysis includes a means-ends schema in two ways. First, means-ends analysis is involved in the conception of the ego-alter interaction as complementarity of role-expectations and as a situation of 'double contingency'; secondly, means-ends approach is involved in the conception of the manner in which a stable ego-alter interaction is established and maintained. The crucial idea here is that of processes as means ('mechanisms') of establishment and maintenance of the equilibrium of social interaction.

SYSTEM-SYSTEM INTERACTION ANALYSIS: PARSONS' MACROFUNCTIONALISM

A means-ends schema, similar to the one involved in ego-alter interaction analysis, is involved in Parsons' fourfold system problem analysis. A basic assumption in this analysis is that the social system has 'needs', 'imperatives' or 'prerequisites' of its own and operates through their satisfaction. Originally Parsons himself did not have a very clear classification of the needs of social systems. In his *Social System*, he states the problem of the system's needs by pointing out that if systems of roles and statuses are 'to constitute a persistent order or undergo any orderly process of developmental change, certain functional prerequisites must be met'.[9] And further, 'a discussion of these functional prerequisites is in order because it provides the setting for a more extended analysis of the points of reference for analysing the structure of social systems.' He goes on to identify these prerequisites:

> First, a social system cannot be so structured as to be radically incompatible with the conditions of functioning of its component individual actors as biological organisms and as personalities, or of the relatively stable integration of a cultural system. Secondly, in turn the social system, on both fronts, depends on the requisite minimum of 'support' from each of the other systems. It must, that is, have a sufficient proportion of its component actors adequately motivated to act in accordance with the requirements of its role system, positively in the fulfilment of expectations and negatively in abstention from too

disruptive, i.e., deviant, behaviour. It must on the other hand avoid commitment to cultural patterns which either fail to define a minimum of order or which place impossible demands on people and thereby generate deviance and conflict to a degree which is incompatible with the minimum conditions of stability or orderly development.[9]

The prerequisites are thus the problems the social system faces in its relation with non-social systems, especially the personality system and the cultural system. The prerequisite of adequate motivation is emphasized as of primary importance, because it gives us a starting point for developing the concepts of role and institutionalization. The prerequisite of adequate motivation has both positive and negative aspects which provide the setting for analysis of the structural problem of the mechanisms of socialization and of social control. Similarly, the cultural prerequisite provides the setting for analysis of the structural problem of communication and of the mechanisms of conformity to cultural patterns when they impose strains both upon the personality and the social systems.[10]

In his *Social System*, however, Parsons' discussion of the functional prerequisites is rather general and not very systematic. Marion Levy has tried to systematize and classify these prerequisites for society in greater detail:

> The list of functional requisites chosen is as follows: (A) provision for an adequate physiological relationship to the setting and for sexual recruitment; (B) role differentiation and role assignment; (C) communication; (D) shared cognitive orientations; (E) a shared articulated set of goals; (F) regulation to the choice of means; (G) regulation of effective expression; (H) adequate socialization; (I) effective control of disruptive forms of behaviour; and (J) adequate institutionalization.[11]

In 1953 Parsons turned his attention to the problem of prerequisites again. Since then he has reduced them to four. Thus,

> I have suggested that it is possible to reduce the essential func-

tional imperatives of any system of action, and hence of any social system, to four, which I have called pattern-maintenance, integration, goal attainment, and adaptation.[12]

Or:

Process in any functional system is subject to four independent functional imperatives or 'problems' which must be met adequately if equilibrium and/or continuing existence of the system is to be maintained.[13]

The imperatives are in effect problems which any social system has to solve. The pattern-maintenance imperative refers to the problem of maintaining the stability of the institutionalized cultural patterns. This is a composite problem. It involves, first, the character of the institutionalized patterns themselves or the content of what is institutionalized, and secondly, the state of institutionalization or the problem of values and maintenance of their stability in the face of the potential sources of their disruption and change to other values.

The second aspect of the problem, also termed the tension management problem, concerns the motivational commitment of the individual to the institutionalized patterns, a commitment to act in accordance with these patterns or values. One very important part of this aspect is the internalization of cultural values, i.e., different ritualistic and symbolic processes.[17]

But although the stability and commitment to the norms and values of society may be maintained, this still does not solve the problem of motivating individuals to contribute their effort to the attainment of any specific goal within a specific situation. It is one thing to be committed to general values, but it is another thing to act in any specific instance even if the goal of this action derives from the general values. Thus, all social systems have also the problem of goal attainment, i.e., the problem of concrete action in specific situations. As Parsons puts it:

Goal attainment then becomes a problem insofar as there arises some discrepancy between the inertial tendencies of the system and its 'needs' resulting from interchange with the situation. Such needs necessarily arise because the internal system and the environing ones cannot be expected to follow immediately the changing patterns of process. A goal is therefore defined in terms of equilibrium. It is a directional change that tends to reduce the discrepancy between the needs of the system, with respect to input-output interchange, and the conditions in the environing systems that bear upon the 'fulfilment' of such needs. Goal-attainment or goal-orientation is thus, by contrast with pattern-maintenance, essentially tied to a specific situation.

The motivational aspect of the problem of goal-attainment is the question of inducing concrete action in accordance with the system's specific goals. As Parsons says,

> for the social system as such, the focus of its goal-orientation lies in its relation as a system to the personalities of the participating individuals. It concerns, therefore, not commitment to the values of the society, but motivation to contribute what is necessary for the functioning of the system; these 'contributions' vary according to particular exigencies.[15]

The imperative of adaptation refers to the problem of mobilizing technical means, or facilities, required for attainment of goals. The important thing is that these facilities be 'disposable', i.e., independent of any particular goal. This, of course, derives from the fact of plurality of goals. Parsons explains:

> With a plurality of goals . . . the problem of 'cost' arises. That is, the same scarce facilities will have alternative uses within the system of goals, and hence their use for one purpose means sacrificing the gains that would have been derived from their use for another. It is on this basis that an analytical distinction must be made between the function of effective goal-attainment and that of providing disposable facilities independent of their relevance to any particular goal. The adaptive function is defined as the provision of such facilities.[16]

In other words, the adaptive problem is that of providing facilities for attainment of goals inasmuch as they remain facilities rather than part of goals themselves. As Parsons states, this means a maximum of generalized disposability of facilities in the process of allocation between alternative uses.

Finally, the imperative of integration refers to the problem of maintaining solidarity of the units of the social system, of holding them in line or insuring their cooperation, despite all the emotional strains involved in the process of goal-attainment and sharing of the fruits of cooperation.[17] It is a sense of solidarity that binds members of a system together and thus integrates the system, or gives it identity. The imperative of integration refers hence to the mutual adjustments of the units, or the subsystems of the system inasmuch as these adjustments 'contribute' to the effective functioning of the system as a whole. It is the problem of allocation of rights and obligations, of facilities and rewards, between the different units of the complex system. This allocation facilitates internal adjustments and hence solidarity within the system.[18]

Such are, according to Parsons, four basic imperatives or needs of the social systems. All the other imperatives mentioned can be, in one way or another, subsumed under these four.

The patterns through which the need satisfaction is effected can be considered as systems themselves, or rather subsystems of the social system. Thus Parsons distinguishes the adaptive subsystem, the goal-attainment subsystem, the integrative subsystem, and the latency subsystem, including pattern-maintenance and tension management. These are analytical systems, but in some degree they correspond to concrete institutional structural systems; this correspondence is especially high in societies in which there is much specialization.[19] For example, Parsons considers the adaptive subsystem as the economy and the goal-attainment subsystem as the polity. Each of these subsystems are social systems in their own right with the same needs which are satisfied through the operation of other subsystems. In this manner the subsystems which are means for satisfaction of the needs of a higher order system are themselves systems with same needs to be satisfied through subsystems of lower orders. The assumption made is that when the subsystems interact 'properly' with one another, then the entire system functions in a balanced equilibrium manner.[20]

The interaction between subsystems takes place through mutual outputs and inputs. The explanation of the sub-system-subsystem interaction parallels the explanation of the ego-alter role interaction. Thus, while in micro-functionalism alter's behaviour is means for satisfaction of ego's need-dispositions, and vice-versa, in macrofunction-alism a subsystem's 'output' is another subsystem's 'input', and vice-versa. Or, a subsystem's production of output for another subsystem makes possible its reception of input from the other subsystem. Similarly to the ego-alter case in which alter's expectations are sanctions for ego's behaviour, a subsystem's input from another subsystem is its sanction for production of output into this other subsystem. The same means-ends schema is employed here. Similarly to the principle of 'double contingency', Parsons calls it the paradigm of 'double interchange'.[21]

Accordingly, the economy's functional output into the polity is productivity; its input from the polity is capital. Its output into the integrative system is 'new output combinations' and its input from the integrative system is 'organization'. The economy's output into the latency system is consumer goods and services; its input from the latter is labour services. The polity's output into the integrative system is 'imperative coordination', and its input— 'contingent support'. Its output into the latency system is allocation of power, and its input, in return, is political loyalty. Finally, the integrative system's output into the latency system is motivation to pattern conformity, and its input from the latency system is the pattern content.[22]

These are rather general categories of the input-output interchange. A more specific analysis of this interchange has been done by Parsons only for the economy.[23] In either case the idea of circularity, by which output is balanced by input, is of basic importance. The meaning of this circularity is that of reciprocity of interest satisfaction. This, however, does not mean symmetry of interests. Parsons does not employ a mechanical model of balance, no matter what the similarities might be. The reciprocity of outputs and inputs is understood by Parsons in the economic sense of the word, in the sense of a *quid pro quo*. In other words, the output makes sense only inasmuch as it takes place for the sake of the input. Each is a sanction for one another. To this extent the logic employed here is the same as in the case of ego-alter 'double contingency' relations; essentially it is the means-ends mode of explanation.

Parsons' interest in economics, however, and his turning to economics to find principles of explanation of the system-system interaction, has added to his sociology a new dimension. It is not that Parsons has decided to subsume the explanation of the behaviour of the social system under economic principles. Rather, he points out that it is possible to generalize economic principles into a logic that is applicable to other types of the social phenomena. Accordingly, a number of economic concepts can be considered as prototypes of other, more strictly sociological, concepts. This has enabled Parsons to develop his macrofunctionalism and to make some new formulations in his social system theory. Among these new formulations is his conception of the subsystems' inputs and outputs as societal resources and that of the process of system-system interchange as a process of allocation, utilization and control of these resources.

The inputs and the outputs of the social subsystems are societal resources analogous to the factors of production in economics, i.e., land, labour, capital, and organization. In addition to the inputs and outputs mentioned above,

Parsons distinguishes what he calls the ultimate resources of society. Unlike the input-output interchanges between the subsystems of the social system, these ultimate resources refer to the input-output interchanges between the social and the contingent non-social systems, i.e., the behavioural organism, personality, and the cultural system.[24] In either case, if a social equilibrium is to be maintained, the processing of these resources, i.e., (1) allocation and (2) utilization of the outputs and inputs among the different systems, must be regulated by a set of mechanisms. Parsons borrows the idea of such mechanisms from economics, specifically the concept of the market and the concept of money. The market regulates allocation of resources, whereas money regulates their utilization. In both cases, the mechanisms work as means of maintaining social equilibrium. Thus, the labour market brings together the employing organizations and the persons seeking employment. The primary operating factor at the market is both the differential and the comparative remuneration. That is, on one hand, different remunerations are offered for different skills, with those jobs requiring more skill offering more remuneration, and on the other hand, on the same skill level remunerations are comparable, so that persons seeking employment have a choice. All this ensures that skills are allocated where they are needed and at the same time that they are allocated between a variety of organizations. In this manner effective allocation of the skill resources is not an accidental occurrence, yet it takes place without any centralized administrative decision.[25]

Parsons applies the same logic to other institutional contexts, especially the political sphere. Thus, allocation of the leadership capacity is effected through a special type of 'labour market' where power is the medium of exchange. Allocation of the leadership capacity is determined through the power market system. To put it in other words, the fact that only some specific rather than just any collectivities acquire leadership capacity is explained not so much in terms of historical antecedents, but in terms of how the leadership capacity, if vested in one group rather than another, would affect the functioning of the entire social system. The specific power market system is therefore the mechanism which makes it possible for leadership to be vested in such collectivity which will not disrupt effective allocation and utilization of other resources like employment, goods, services, etc. Consequently, the specific allocation of leadership within a social system is not just a product of historical circumstances, much less an accident, but a means to an end, the end being the societal equilibrium. Parsons emphasizes that societal equilibrium in this context means 'normal' operation of the social system as a whole, as distinguished from the question of equilibrium involved in social change.[26]

The mechanisms regulating utilization of societal resources can also find their prototypes in economics, especially in the form of money. The important thing about money is that it is a generalized medium. That is,

> the household which sells the labour of a member to a firm through employment does not ordinarily purchase most of the goods it consumes from the employing firm. The relations are mediated through money so that the exchanges, from the point of view of the household are: (1) labour for money (wages), and (2) money (through consumers' spending) for goods. From the point of view of the firm, the exchanges are: (1) proceeds (in money) from the sale of goods, and (2) wage payments in exchange for labour services. Money mediates the transactions as a 'measure of value' and as a medium of exchange.[27]

Money, hence, is a means of maintenance of social equilibrium at least in two ways. First, it enables the units of interaction in the economic system i.e., the households, to obtain the goods they consume from a variety of sources rather than only from the employing firm. This makes possible maintenance of a system in which interdependence of a variety of units is the rule, i.e., a specialized and a differentiated system. Without some such generalized medium of exchange, a system of this type could hardly be conceived to function at all.

Secondly, money ties together different levels of organizational structures within society. It connects the organization of the household consumption with that of the physical production of goods and with that of the managerial decision-making level. Here again it makes possible maintenance of a system in which differentiation of levels of organization of activity is the most significant characteristic.

In both cases money is instrumental in maintaining equilibrium. But Parsons finds mechanisms which function in the same manner as money in other areas of social life. In the political realm, 'power' can be said to be the medium of exchange. However,

> this time the interchange is between political parties and the members of the voting 'public' (United States example). Just as firms bid for labour services in the labour market, so parties, through their candidates and in other ways, bid for generalized political support. What the public gets in return, very unevenly distributed and highly particularized, is 'binding decisions' on the part of government which eventually settle many issues and allocate many benefits and burdens throughout the society.[28]

Power passes from the electorate to a specific 'leader', who in return is bound to produce political decisions that ultimately benefit the voting public.

Like money, power functions to maintain social equilibrium in two ways. First, it enables the voters to 'buy' political decisions from a variety of leaderships, and thus helps to maintain a politically differentiated society. Secondly, it binds together two levels of the social structure, the cultural and the associational. It involves commitment of the leadership to the ideological platforms which express the specific interests of the supporting interest groups.

Parsons also applies the economic logic of money to the teacher-student relationships where 'rewards' and 'readiness to learn' are the media of exchange. The almost aesthetic value of this logic in all the cases lies in its basic premise that as long as the given medium is circulating within the system, the system's resources are being utilized through inputs and outputs and its equilibrium is being maintained. Any change in the circulation process of the medium has a disequilibrating effect. Thus, in the case of money, disequilibrium occurs when either there is not enough money in circulation due to oversaving or underspending,—i.e., 'deflation', or there is an addition of money in circulation—'inflation'.

In the case of politics, 'political deflation' may be said to derive from one or both of two sources: (1) political 'oversaving', which takes place when the 'public' fails to put forth sufficient 'demands' for political action relative to its previous 'income' from such action; and (2) 'undercommitment on the part of party leadership so that, relative to potential support, they . . . (do) not take sufficiently bold initiative'.[29] On the other hand, 'political inflation' would result

> from 'overdemands' for decisions relative to the capacity of the political system to produce them in adequate 'quality' (i.e., as genuinely binding); or from (2) overcommitment on the part of leadership relative to potential support (i.e., claiming capacities to 'satisfy' that support which could not be fulfilled).[29]

In either case, political deflation or political inflation produces a disequilibrium as a result of changes in the circulation of power between the 'public' and the political leadership relative to the previous state of the political system. The same applies to the educational system where 'rewards and readiness to learn' is the circulating medium.[30]

It is at this point that a problem arises. Although it can be said that a specific medium of exchange is instrumental in maintaining a system's equilibrium and thus its persistence can be explained, it cannot be said that a specific medium is instrumental in occurence of disequilibrium. Media of exchange make possible smooth utilization of resources, but have nothing to do with the question of whether the resources would be utilized at all. Any deflation or inflation is a sign of changes in the circulation process of the media, but cannot be explained by the media themselves. Utilization of resources ultimately is not causally necessitated by the system's equilibrium, but depends upon other factors. The latter basically involve decision to employ the media and commit the specific resources for utilization. As Parsons says in regard to money:

> The significant point is that possessing money involves a power or capacity to get things done, while *avoiding* specific commitments at the moment—i.e., about specific channels of expenditure in terms of object or of source of supply, about time of purchase, and about price. The combination of effectiveness (purchasing power) and freedom from commitment makes money such an important mechanism. Spending money is like speaking: the utterance, once made, has consequences; but the speaker who commands a language and has certain knowledge he can formulate in its terms retains his freedom to say what he likes until he is committed through acts of utterance.[31]

Employing his economic analogy, Parsons thus arrives at another new formulation in his theory, that of decision-making. Accordingly, utilization of societal resources is essentially a process of 'successively more particularized decision-making'. That is, utilization of resources refers to the question of control over resource-units by their recipients, and the control involves the recipients' decision of either to 'consume' the units or to transfer them to other uses. Therefore, any social 'inflation' or 'deflation' will be ultimately effected through the recipients' decision-making.

It is interesting to note that implied here is a means-ends schema of a type different from that in the above discussion. Parsons points out that a medium of exchange, e.g., money, can function either as a facility or as a reward. When it functions as a facility, it can be said to be viewed by the one who controls it as a means to future rewards. On the other hand, when it functions as a reward, the medium of exchange can be said to be considered as an end in itself. Thus, to the extent a medium of exchange is considered by the 'public' as means only, that is, it is being put into circulation immediately, to that extent an inflationary effect is produced. On the other hand, to the extent the medium is viewed as a relative end, that is, its circulation is delayed through saving, to that extent a deflationary effect is produced.

But returning to the media of social exchange as being the mechanisms of social equilibrium, the fact that utilization of resources is not causally necessitated by the system's equilibrium also means that the system's equilibrium cannot be said to productively cause the mechanisms through which resources are utilized. Yet, the equilibrium can explain the persistence of the mechanisms by the argument that they persist because they make the equilibrium possible. This is, of course, a form of telecausal explanation.

Emphasis on decision-making as comprising the process of utilization of societal resources is intertwined with another new formulation of Parsons', that of conceiving the subsystem-subsystem interaction as a cybernetic process. Thus, if utilization of resources is a process of decision-making, decision-making itself is governed by the process of transmission of information. The latter produces a hierarchical order of control between the different social subsystems, so that one subsystem controls the actions of another because it feeds into it the information necessary for its utilization of resources.[32] In this manner, the four social subsystems form a chain of cybernetic control through which utilization of societal resources is accomplished. In this chain the pattern-maintenance subsystem is first, the integrative subsystem second, the goal-attainment subsystem third, and the adaptive subsystem last. Utilization of resources can thus be seen as a series of 'circuits' of action, beginning in the pattern-maintenance subsystem and ending in the adaptive subsystem. Each 'circuit' is a process of committing resources to the accomplishment of a specific task. Once the task is accomplished, the process ends and then begins all over again in view of a new task. As Parsons says:

There is in the operation of the social system, a *terminus ad quem* of the process, i.e., the ultimate accomplishment of tasks. This may be defined as the point at which no further commitment of societal resources is required as 'reasonable' in that particular task-context. For example, maintaining an elderly person is an institutionalized social obligation. On his death, however, the obligation of maintenance is terminated and the tasks of relatives, health-care personnel, etc. involved are completed, except for the function of funeral observance, settlement of a possible estate, etc. The resources previously committed to this task are, if still unconsumed, freed for another.[33]

Accomplishment of the specific task is thus not simply a cessation of the resource-utilization process, but an end in view of which the entire process is to be understood. The process would make little sense if no task were to be accomplished.[34]

In summary, Parsons' macrofunctionalism involves a means-ends schema in (1) his notion of the needs of the social system; these needs become *explananses* of the social process; (2) his conception of the 'double interchange' between the subsystems, especially in the form of inputs and outputs; (3) the mechanisms, such as the market, money, power, etc. through which societal resources are allocated and utilized; (4) in his final conception of the total process of functioning of the social system as the cybernetic process.

Chapter V

THE EXPLANATORY IMPORT
OF FUNCTIONALISM:
OBJECTIONS AND EVALUATION

The preceding chapters have attempted to show that
functionalist explanation includes both productively causal
as well as telecausal explanation. As was already mentioned,
many commentators on functionalism admit that functionalism has an appearance of 'teleological' explanation, but
most of them will also agree that it is only an appearance,
and that functionalist explanatory import is not teleological.
Rather, the argument goes, all teleological formulations in
functionalism can be substituted by non-teleological statements without any loss in content. The most outstanding
proponent of this idea has been Ernest Nagel.[1] Since his
argument is often cited when the issue of teleology in functionalism is raised, it will be opportune to analyse his
argument in some detail.

THE QUESTION OF REDUCTION OF
TELECAUSALITY TO PRODUCTIVE CAUSALITY:
ERNEST NAGEL'S ARGUMENT

Nagel's argument is indeed very simple. He summarizes it
succintly in one paragraph. He states:

> It seems that when a function is ascribed to a constituent of
> some organism, the content of the teleological statement is
> fully conveyed by another statement which simply asserts a
> necessary (or possibly a necessary and sufficient) condition for

a certain trait or activity of that organism. On this assumption, therefore, a teleological explanation states the *consequences* for a given biological system of one of the latter's constituent parts or processes; the equivalent non-teleological explanation states some of the *conditions* ... under which the system persists in its characteristic organization and activities. The difference between teleological and non-teleological explanations is thus comparable to the difference between saying that B is an effect of A, and saying that A is a cause or condition of B. In brief, the difference is one of selective attention, rather than of asserted content.[2]

Nagel illustrates his argument by stating that the teleological statement 'the function of chlorophyll in plants is to enable plants to perform photosynthesis', asserts nothing which is not asserted by the non-teleological statement 'plants perform photosynthesis only if they contain chlorophyll', or alternatively, 'a necessary condition for the occurence of photosynthesis in plants is the presence of chlorophyll.'

It is interesting to note that many sociologists who have acclaimed Nagel's argument have never bothered to analyse its logic.[3] For, somehow, Nagel has failed to admit the logical flaw in his own argument; his teleological and his non-teleological statements do not 'fully convey' the same content and are not equivalent. Close examination of what each statement conveys shows the difference between the two. Thus, the statement 'plants perform photosynthesis only if they contain chlorophyll' says:

1. Plants can perform photosynthesis.
2. Chlorophyll is necessary for photosynthesis in plants.
3. Without chlorophyll plants cannot perform photosynthesis.

On the other hand, the statement 'the function of chlorophyll in plants is to enable plants to perform photosynthesis', says:

1. Chlorophyll has a function.
2. This function is to enable plants to perform photosynthesis.
3. Plants can perform photosynthesis.

But it *does not* say in any way that:

Without chlorophyll plants cannot perform photosynthesis.

In other words, the first statement, which is a productively causal statement, involves *necessity* between chlorophyll and photosynthesis, whereas the second statement, which is a telecausal statement, does not. The latter statement allows for substitutes of chlorophyll, the former does not.

Nagel realizes that the second statement does not convey the idea of necessity. Yet, he states that although it is theoretically possible for green plants to maintain themselves without chlorophyll, there is no evidence whatsoever showing that they do so in their actual mode of organization. Hence, since teleological analysis is not merely an exploration in logical possibilities but deals with actual functions of definite components of concrete living systems, if a process is known to be indispensable in a given system, then it can also be said to be necessary for the maintenance of the system. In effect, teleological explanation does not differ in content from non-teleological explanations.[4]

Nevertheless, Nagel's argument remains unconvincing especially when indispensability of a component of a system cannot be assumed, as is the case particularly in the social system. In either case, however, the fact remains that, as such, the two statements about chlorophyll and photosynthesis not only do not say the same thing, but on the contrary, express two rather different ideas.

In the first statement, chlorophyll is a necessary antecedent of photosynthesis, in the second statement, it is a means of photosynthesis. The implied meaning of the word function is that of directed action, i.e., action directed to occurrence of photosynthesis. The first statement does not imply such action; it implies only the notion of necessity.[5]

EVALUATION OF THE COMMON OBJECTIONS
TO TELECAUSALITY

The objections to the use of telecausal explanations in

science are concerned primarily with two things, (1) that imputation of ends to phenomena other than individual human beings is, in effect, anthropomorphism and cannot be tested empirically, and (2) that to consider phenomena as acting toward ends is to employ value-judgments.[6]

From the point of view of logic, neither of these objections justifies a wholesale rejection of telecausality as a useful form of scientific explanation. In regard to the first objection, too often action directed towards an end is confused with purpose or intention of the subject of action.[7] The two are not the same. It is one thing to say that things act for a purpose—it is another thing to say that they act toward an end. As was explained above, telecausality does not necessarily imply subjective intention or purpose, and the telecausality of functionalism is not primarily concerned with intended action.

If, however, the notion of directed action still remains anthropomorphic, then we can legitimately ask the question as to what concepts in the methodological tool-kit of science are not anthropomorphic? In no way is the concept of directed action more anthropomorphic than are the notions of necessity and sufficiency, or even those of the antecedent and the consequent. Neither necessity nor sufficiency can be proven empirically, and yet most philosophers of science today, including Nagel himself, would deny that a scientific law is nothing more than a simple empirical generalization. Thus, one representative of the Neo-Positivist thought, A. J. Ayer, recalls that Hume had recognized the impossibility of discovering in the operations of causes the idea of 'necessary connection', i.e., 'any quality which binds the effect to the cause, and renders the one an infallible consequence of the other'.[8] This idea, according to Hume, is not a copy of any sense impression, yet it somehow must be derived from experience. His solution is that when one observes repeatedly two events occurring together, the mind is carried by habit, upon the appearance of an event, to expect its usual attendant, and to believe that it will exist. Hence, as a result of this repetition, man comes to feel the events to be connected in his imagination. Ayer disagrees with Hume and denies that even the experience of repetition of events is involved in the origin of the idea of necessity. He says:

> Now if our purpose were to give to the expression 'necessary connexion' a meaning that would be substantially in accordance with ordinary usage, but would, at the same time, make it refer only to what was capable of being observed, Hume's theory could, with certain slight modifications, be regarded as acceptable. But if the theory is designed, as seems to be the case, to account for the origin of the belief that there attaches to the events themselves a quality or relation 'which binds the effect to the cause', it is plainly inadequate. It may perhaps explain how we pass from the recognition that in all the cases, hitherto observed, events of the kind A have been succeeded by events of the kind B, to a belief that they are, in fact, conjoined in all cases; but it does not at all account for the assumption that instances of B *must* always follow instances of A, as distinct from the assumption that they actually always have, and always will. How then are we to explain this use of the word 'must'? The answer is, I think, that it is either a relic of animism, or else reveals an inclination to treat causal connexion as if it were a form of logical necessity. These two explanations are not, indeed, psychologically exclusive of one another. It is arguable, for instance, that the attempt to assimilate causality to logical entailment is, on the part of some philosophers, a rationalization of an unconcious animistic belief in 'necessary connexion'. But they are at any rate logically distinct.[9]

Ayer argues further that to assume that necessity is a 'real tendency' in the observed phenomena is to adopt a hypothesis that cannot in any way be verified. And if without a hypothesis of this kind it is impossible to justify causal inference, then any demand for the justification of causal inference is itself unjustifiable. Necessity is ultimately an idea borrowed from the human moral world and Ayer concludes:

Accordingly, the question which must be put to those who speak as if there were necessity in nature is whether they really mean to imply that the laws of nature are normative rules, enforced by a divine will. If they do not mean to imply this, their talk of necessity is at best an unfortunate metaphor. If they mean to imply it, then not only are they assigning to what have been assumed to be 'scientific' terms a meaning that is at variance with modern scientific usage; but, what is far more serious, they are interpreting causal propositions in such a way that they can have no valid reason whatsoever for believing any of them to be true.[10]

Though less sceptical about the value of causal explanation, Morris Cohen and Ernest Nagel also point out that the methods used by science to either prove or demonstrate productive causality and the ideas of necessity and sufficiency implied in it are not capable of doing either. They write:

> The experimental methods are neither methods of proof nor methods of discovery. The canons which formulate them state in a more explicit manner what it is we generally *understand* by a causal and invariant relation. They *define* what we mean by the relation of cause and effect, but do not *find* cases of such a relation. The hope of discovering a method that will 'leave little to the sharpness and strength of men's wits' is one which finds no support from a careful study of the procedure of the sciences.[11]

Yet, paradoxically, Cohen and Nagel assert that the goal of science is to find the conditions of phenomena which are both necessary and sufficient, even if this goal may never be reached.[12] Whether either necessity or sufficiency can be proven or not, there seems to be an agreement among a good number of logicians of science that simple empirical generalizations which do not go beyond the observable data are not enough for science. Valuable scientific knowledge is derived from propositions which are not simply empirically substantiated, but which can be regarded as laws because they allow either deductive inferences or are themselves deducible from other propositions. Scientists look for laws because laws *explain*. And laws explain because they permit deduction. As R. B. Braithwaite says:

> A hypothesis to be regarded as a natural law must be a general proposition which can be thought to *explain* its instances; if the reason for believing the general proposition is solely direct knowledge of the truth of its instances, it will be felt to be a poor sort of explanation of those instances. If, however, there is evidence for it which is independent of its instances, such as the indirect evidence provided by instances of a same-level general proposition subsumed along with it under the same higher-level hypothesis, then the general proposition will *explain* its instances in the sense that it will provide grounds for believing in that truth independently of any direct knowledge of such truth. . . . The case for accepting any particular higher-level hypothesis containing theoretical concepts is exactly that it serves as an explanation of the lower-level generalizations deducible from it, whereas the case for accepting a particular generalization not containing theoretical concepts and not deducible from any higher-level hypothesis is the fact that it covers its known instances rather than that it explains them.[13]

The essence of deduction, however, is not the derivation of particular conclusions from universal propositions, but as Cohen and Nagel have pointed out, it is the derivation of conclusions which are *necessarily* involved in the premises.[14] It is thus the elements which are not empirically provable, be it necessity in any of its senses or sufficiency, that provide the explanatory import in science. By the same argument, there is no reason why telecausality should be rejected from science on the grounds of its empirical non-provability, if it is able to provide explanatory import not provided by other methods.

In regard to the use of value-judgments in functionalism, when we speak about a part which as an end of its activity contributes to the maintenance of the whole rather than to its disruption, are we not evaluating that part? The answer seems to be affirmative. To the extent that telecausality involves discrimination of the phenomena which are relevant to the maintenance of the system, to that extent a certain value-judgment is made.[15] Harold Fallding has gone so far as to take the position that because of the teleology involved in functionalism, functionalism is not concerned with explanation but only with evaluation. He says:

> Does not the anticipation of an end to be achieved underlie all our judgments of function or dysfunction, when those judgments are made in such a way as to imply a comparison with the alternative possible outcome? In the writer's view, what we are interested in *when we make this comparison* is not explanation but evaluation.[16]

In other words, evaluation in functionalism is involved in the ideas of 'maintenance', 'integration', 'contribution', 'support', 'fulfilment of needs'. All of these imply a positive-negative polarity. Does this mean then that the functionalist method is basically subjective, allowing varying private interpretations? Fallding answers in the negative and points out that, on the contrary, functional method is objective because the criteria of evaluation are not anybody's biases, but the social needs postulated for the social system.

It is in this manner that the problem of value-judgments in functionalism derives from its assumption of a model of a self-regulating system and, as was shown earlier, self-regulation is the key idea in telecausality. Yet, Fallding, following Braithwaite, points out that 'where a need-satisfaction stands at the end of a process of human endeavour it exercises some directive power over the efforts taken to achieve it', i.e., the end of the process has a determining power over the process itself. There is, therefore, no need to consider what Fallding calls 'objective evaluation' as non-explanatory methodology. To the extent that determinacy is involved, any methodology is explanatory analysis.[17] It is not true, as Fallding says, that functionalists are not interested in explanation, only evaluation. On the contrary, functionalists' concern has been more with explaining persistence of certain patterns of behaviour than with simply evaluating them as either functional or dysfunctional.[18]

Of course, to steer clear of all or any value-judgments we could reject the model of a self-regulating system. From the standpoint of logic there is nothing which tells us that we should assume a model of a self-regulating system, but there is also nothing which tells us that it should be rejected. It is hence a question of methodological values; ultimately, a question of fruitfulness of the approach. Much of sociological research has involved only productive causality, and, as was pointed out above, Mertonian version of functionalism tends to restrict itself to an assumption of a non-self-regulating system. But if assumption of a self-regulating system will give us more insight, there is no reason other than the methodological bias why it should be excluded from legitimate theory construction and research.

We are not implying that the model of telecausal system is equally applicable to all phenomena. Indeed, it seems that its applicability is much more limited than that of productively causal models. But this limitation of the telecausal model does not mean that it should not be applied whenever such application can be fruitful. The only justification for a choice or rejection of a methodological approach is the probability it offers of a fruitful investigation and knowledge. As Paul Hanly Furfey has stated,

A new research technique can be examined and be judged promising. To assert this is to make a metasociological value judgment concerning useful values and to make it merely with probability. As the technique is carried out by different investigators under different circumstances, however, the uncertainty is gradually reduced until the procedure is so well understood that the experienced sociologist knows with certainty, or with something approaching certainty, just where it is applicable and what type of results it can be expected to yield. At the present time there are a number of divergent schools advocating different methodological approaches to sociology. It is impossible to decide with certainty among the conflicting claims. Yet there is every reason to believe that experience will clear up the uncertainties, the relative usefulness of different methodologies will be clarified, and the area of disagreement will be gradually and constantly narrowed. The test of practical experience is often exasperatingly slow, but it is excellent.[19]

We conclude, therefore, that the objections to tele-causality in science and especially its wholesale rejection from the scientific domain is in essence ideological rather than logical. This methodological ideology has been fostered in particular by the followers of the Vienna Circle.[20] Indeed, the Circle has produced logicians and methodologists who have highly developed the logic of science, especially the logical problems connected with productive causality, but it is unfortunate that the Circle's methodological ideology has become the vogue for the philosophers of science. No doubt the original positions of the Circle have changed, many followers have moved away from pure positivism, yet, a certain disregard of telecausal approach has remained.[21] On the other hand, those who favour the use of more biological models and telecausal explanations so far have not developed a logic comparable in sophistication to the contributions of the Vienna Circle.[22] Nevertheless, fruitful employment of telecausal explanation, especially in sociology, gives hope for the future development of its logic.

THE USE OF ORGANISMIC MODEL

Both intercausality and telecausality are rooted in the idea of an 'organismic' system assumed by functionalism. It is this assumption that distinguishes functionalism from other forms of explanation in sociology. Kingsley Davis, however, in a now famous presidential address, has denied that functionalism is any special method or theory in sociology. He says that beneath the myth of the label of functionalism one can find a body of theory and research that is synonymous with sociology itself. Any scientific discipline, says Davis, assumes 'a *system* of reasoning which presumably bears a relation to a corresponding *system* in nature', and the least that any science could do is to relate the parts to the whole. Similarly, the 'feedback' idea assumed by functionalism is for Davis nothing which is not assumed by any scientific analysis. Thus:

> How else can data be interpreted except in relation to the larger structures *in which they are implicated*? How can data on the earth's orbit, for example, be understood except in relation to a system in which they are involved—in this case, the solar system or the earth's climatic system? Since in science some kind of system is being dealt with, an analysis of the effect of one factor must always be made with the possibility in mind of a possible return effect ('feedback') on that factor itself. If, for example, the increase of fish (y) in a pond has the effect of increasing the toxicity (x) of the water, the growth of the fish population (y again) will eventually cease unless other factors intervene. This is not explaining things solely by their consequences, but rather by the way their consequences react upon them. [23]

Unfortunately, the system that Davis talks about is not the type assumed by functionalism, at least the Parsonian version of it. Perhaps some system must be assumed by all science but there are different types of systems. Davis really talks about a mechanical system. What he describes as the return effect is not the same as the idea of self-regulation. Davis talks about a chain of productive causality. To put the explanation in the context of a self-regulating system, one would have to phrase the problem in this fashion: the increase of fish in a pond has the effect of increasing the toxicity of the water, yet there are mechanisms within the fish-pond system itself which prevent the toxicity from increasing to such an extent as to stop the growth of the fish population. Indeed, it is doubtful whether the concept of a self-regulating system would be applicable to the fish-pond situation. Davis says that there must be other factors or else the growth of the fish population will cease, but he does not say whether these other factors are internal or external to the system, or whether there is any form of equilibrium. It is noteworthy that Davis never discusses the idea of equilibrium. Yet, the notion of equilibrium is essential for the conception of a self-regulating system.[24]

Assumption of the self-regulating system, just like assumption of any methodological technique, must be somehow justifiable. Assumptions can be justifiable on different grounds, depending upon their specific type. If we use the term assumption in a generic sense, then we can distinguish at least between such specific types of assumptions as postulates, hypotheses, and models.

Postulates can be considered as propositions which are accepted as premises for deduction and therefore become, an integral part of theory. Postulates can be of several types. First, a distinction can be made between formal and nonformal postulates. Formal postulates are propositions in which no assumption is made as to their factual truth. That is, the relation between the predicables of such a proposition can be purely arbitrary without any reference to its truth value. The use of formal postulates is justifiable on the grounds that they make a discourse or an argument possible. Without them a specific argument whose value consists in logical relations could not be presented.

Nonformal postulates, on the other hand, refer to propositions which are assumed to be true to fact. This is assumed either because the proposition's truth is considered to be self-evident, or because it is presumed to be proved elsewhere. In the first case, an example can be the proposition 'if A is equal to B, and B is equal to C, then "obviously" A is equal to C'. Postulates of this type are also known as axioms.[25] In the second case the proposition is considered to be *demonstrable,* though the discourse which employs this proposition is not concerned with its demonstration. Of course, there could be a number of ways of demonstrating the truth of a proposition, ranging from non-empirical and indirect empirical demonstrations to direct empirical demonstration. But probably most propositions assumed as 'demonstrable' postulates cannot be demonstrated in a direct empirical way. Examples can be such propositions as 'nature is orderly and regular', 'human beings have the subconscious', 'all human beings enter into social relations', and the like.[26] The use of postulates is justifiable because they allow deduction of other propositions, among them hypotheses to be tested by empirical research, and in this way they make possible construction of substantive theories.

A hypothesis is a proposition which is not assumed to be true, but only *probably* true. It is, therefore, not a premise of a discourse which aims at producing new knowledge through deduction, but a tentative assumption in a discourse which aims at assessing its truth. Once its truth gets to be assessed with enough certainty, then the proposition stops being an assumption within the discourse and becomes its conclusion. On the other hand, a hypothesis can always be rejected, that is, the conclusion of the discourse can be rejection of the hypothesis as false. Assumption of a hypothesis, therefore, is justifiable on the grounds of the probability of its verification.[27] There is, of course, also a relation between verification of hypotheses and postulates of a theory. If a hypothesis which is either deduced or deducible from a postulate of a theory is rejected as false, then this puts into question the value of the postulate itself within the theory.

A model is not a proposition but a set of propositions logically connected with one another. These propositions are not assumed as true to facts studied within an area of discourse, but are assumed because they refer to facts which are considered similar to those studied within the area of discourse. The assumption is that if the set of propositions explains facts within one universe of discourse, it *might* also explain similar facts within another universe of discourse. The propositions do not *really* become premises for deduction of truth about a particular subject matter, but they remain conditional ('as if') premises for deduction of *conditional* truth ('as if' truth) about that subject matter. The knowledge ultimately gained is not one which derives from deduction or empirical verification, but from *correspondence* of propositions between two areas of discourse. May Brodbeck has called this correspondence *isomorphism*. Accordingly, one theory can serve as a model of another theory, if it can be made isomorphic with it. As she puts it:

> Suppose that one area, as indicated by a set of descriptive concepts, for which a relatively well developed theory is at hand is said to be a model for another area, about which little is yet known. The descriptive terms in the theory of the better-known area are put into one-by-one correspondence with those of the new area. By means of this one-to-one correspondence, the laws of one area are 'translated' into laws of the other area. The concepts of the better known theory are replaced in the laws by the concepts of the new area. This replacement results in a set of laws or hypotheses about the variables of the new area. If observation shows these hypotheses to be true, then the laws of both areas have the same form. The lawful connections are preserved and the two theories are completely isomorphic to each other. For example, suppose it is wondered whether rumours spread like diseases. That is, can the laws of epidemiology, about which quite a bit is known, be a model for a theory of rumour transmission? Or, to say the same thing differently, do the laws about rumours have the same form as the laws about diseases? The descriptive concepts in the laws of epidemiology are first of all replaced by letter variables. This reveals the form of the laws. The concepts referring to diseases are put into one-to-one correspondence with those referring to rumours. The letter variables in the epidemiological laws are replaced by the descriptive terms referring to rumours. This results in a set of hypotheses about rumours, which may or may not be confirmed. If, optimistically, these laws are confirmed, then the two theories have the same form.[28]

The value of a model depends not upon the truth value of its propositions but upon the logical connections between them. In other words, a scientific model is a ready-made theory applied to an area where a theory is lacking. These are the grounds which justify the use of a model of any type.

Its value is heuristic. It directs and organizes research, it shows how a theory is to be built and even if the propositions of the model are ultimately substituted by others which are not isomorphic with them, nevertheless the model, through its logic, provides scaffolding for the connection between these new propositions, as well as suggests what type of propositions to look for.

The question pertinent to our study is what type of assumption is the functionalist assumption of a self-regulating system. It has been called all three, a set of postulates, a hypothesis, and a model.[29] It is difficult to give one answer to this question. Functionalist assumption of the self-regulating system is a combination of assumptions, most notably postulates and those of a model. We can say the assumption is a rather generalized model taken from biology with some of its propositions postulated as real premises.

The basic elements or propositions of the model are the following: (1) integration of diverse elements into a unity, (2) interdependence of these elements, so that they can be treated as variables, (3) self-regulation, as represented by the notion of equilibrium, (4) presence of needs of the whole system, (5) processes of need-satisfaction. All these together form the basic heuristics of functionalism: explaining the diverse elements as either acting towards integration or disintegration of the unit.

As can be readily seen, these propositions refer to a biological organism, but they refer to rather generalized aspects of it. There are no propositions referring to specific biological systems, like the circulatory system, the nervous system, the digestive system, etc. This is one thing which distinguishes contemporary functionalism from the old organicism in sociology of the Spencerian type. Furthermore, it can be safely said that in the functionalist literature at least propositions (1) and (2) are accepted and treated as postulates. Indeed, proposition (1) is the basic proposition of the entire model and the cornerstone of functionalism.

Because these propositions are assumed as postulates from which deductions are made, functionalism is more than just a method of inquiry; it is also a substantive theory. In this it is akin to the old organicism. It is unfair to functionalism to consider it, as some writers do, as only a methodology. Hempel, for example, considers functionalism as simply of heuristic value. This might be so if one considers functionalism, as he does, in the abstract, as applicable either to biology, psychology, or sociology. In the abstract, it remains a model methodology. In terms of specific disciplines, however, one has to examine the literature to see to what extent propositions of a model are accepted also as postulates.[30]

Since postulates are held to be demonstrable, the question remains as to whether the postulates of integration and interdependence are in any way demonstrable. If they are, then they can be considered as plausible or appropriate. It should be remarked again that functionalism itself is not concerned with demonstrating the truth of these postulates, although, as was mentioned already, there is an indirect relation between fruitful research and appropriateness of postulates.

The problem of plausibility of the postulate of integration and interdependence of the social phenomena has been an important reason why many sociologists have had reservations about functionalism. Robert Merton has actually rejected the postulate as not demonstrable and, in effect, has been reluctant to accept the model of a self-regulating system as valuable for functionalism. As he says:

> One need not go far afield to show that the assumption of the complete functional unity of human society is repeatedly contrary to fact. Social usages or sentiments may be functional for some groups and dysfunctional for others in the same society. Anthropologists often cite 'increased solidarity of the community' and 'increased family pride' as instances of functionally adaptive sentiments. Yet, as Bateson among others has indicated, an increase of pride among individual families may often

serve to disrupt the solidarity of a small local community. Not only is the postulate of functional unity often contrary to fact, but it has little heuristic value, since it diverts the analyst's attention from possible disparate consequences of a given social or cultural item (usage, belief, behaviour pattern, institution) for diverse social groups and for the individual members of these groups.[31]

Merton concludes by saying that the unity of society cannot be usefully posited, that observation does not really bear it out and any theory based on this postulate becomes too one-sided.

Davis and Dore concur with Merton. Davis states that it would be silly to regard the proposition that societies are perfectly integrated as literally true, and Dore points out that any modification of the proposition from 'always perfectly' to 'usually somewhat' integrated destroys the possibility of its empirical falsification and therefore renders the proposition valueless.[32]

An argument often given is that the postulate of integration is applicable to non-literate aboriginal societies, but not to contemporary, changing, individualistic societies; those who developed functionalism in the social sciences have been anthropologists; therefore this is the reason why the postulate remained when attention shifted to modern societies. J. H. M. Beattie puts it this way:

The classical field studies of Malinowski and Radcliffe-Brown were undertaken among small island communities. Since it appeared that these societies were functioning in much the same way as they had always functioned . . . for these first intensive field-workers a synchronic, functional approach was wholly consistent with the nature of their social material. . . . But so simple a recipe (as functionalism) proved inadequate . . . for the understanding of the more complex western societies, to the study of which social anthropologists have recently turned. For it was plain that these were anything but integrated working wholes, and their complexity could not be adequately comprehended in so restricted a frame of reference. Theories and hypotheses associated with the functional approach have had, therefore, ... to submit to review and revision.[33]

Merton's rejection of this postulate represents one such revision in American sociology. Parsons represents another. Parsons, however, retains the postulate of integration. But it would be erroneous to interpret social integration as a condition in which all parts of the social system work together in harmony or internal consistency, without producing persistent conflicts. Most criticism of the postulate of integration refers to this interpretation of it.[34] But such interpretation is completely misleading as far as Parsonian type of functionalism is concerned. The more proper meaning of the postulate is that of society functioning as a unit, even if the parts of the unit are in conflict with one another rather than in harmony. The idea of integration of society cannot be understood without the notion of equilibrium. Within this context conflict or tendency to deviance can be seen as 'normal' processes. Nevertheless, these processes do not lead to disruption of the unit, although they can; but as long as they do not, the unit is said to remain in a functioning equilibrium. Or vice versa, as long as an equilibrium is maintained in spite of any conflict or deviance, the unit remains integrated. The Parsonian meaning of the idea of social integration is that of an equilibrating unity. If this still involves a notion of order and consistency (even by definition any unity of diverse elements implies ordering of these elements), then this is a postulate not typical of functionalism only, but as Davis rightly pointed out, a postulate commonly accepted in sociology as a whole. The alternative would be sociological nominalism—denial that society is a unit in any real sense. This is precisely Dore's position; he calls it, after J. W. N. Watkins, 'methodological individualism', which, in effect, is reductionism of sociology to psychology.[35] But this is not specifically the functionalist issue. The functionalist meaning of the notion of integration derives from the other propositions of the 'organismic' model, especially that of self-regulation. The proper functionalist issue is not whether it is justifiable to assume that society is an ordered, harmonious whole, but whether it is justifiable to assume that in view of all the observable conflicting elements and processes, society can be said to function as a unit. There are empirical grounds that can somewhat justify this assumption. The fact that divergent processes coexist, the fact that they can be shown to be interdependent, the fact that events within society can be shown to influence all the divergent elements within it, all this makes the postulate of integration plausible. At any rate, in Parsonian functionalism, the proposition of integration of society into a functioning unity is accepted much more seriously than on an 'as if' basis.

Perhaps it would contribute to more theoretical precision if one would stay away from postulating propositions of a model. Yet, postulation of propositions of a model can help to formulate significant theoretical problems and thus help develop substantive theory. The value of any model or postulates is ultimately determined by the fruitfulness of the theory they produce, that is by their explanatory import, both in terms of formulation of problems and in terms of their solution.

Before summarizing the explanatory value of functionalism, I will take up George C. Homans' recent critique of functionalism. Homans' critique is another example of methodological individualism, but unlike Dore's position, it centres around an emphasis on the deductive nature of scientific explanations.

GEORGE C. HOMANS' CRITIQUE OF FUNCTIONALISM

Homans' argument briefly stated is that structural functional theory is not a unique theory in sociology, because all its propositions ultimately are derivable from some psychological proposition about individual human beings. As he put it:

The actions of a man that we take to be evidence of his personality are not different from his actions that, together with the actions of others, make up a social system. They are the same identical actions. The theorist will realize this when he finds that the same set of general propositions are needed for explaining the phenomena of both personality and society.[36]

In another essay he states:

The position taken here does not rob sociologists of their subject-matter. There is nothing in it to prevent sociologists, other than some kinds of theorists, from doing what they have always done, especially as the psychologists will not be doing it. Let them go on producing theories like the one of Durkheim's. . . . The fact that their theories may be open at the top, that their highest-order propositions may ultimately be derivable from psychological propositions, does not make the theories invalid. Indeed, I see no great reason why any sociologist should worry at all about 'general' theory except under one condition. If sociologists come along, as they do, telling me that theirs is a general theory and that it is structural-functional, I am a mere dog in a manger, though I may be correct, when I simply deny there is any general theory. To be constructive, I must put forward an alternative. The only main type of alternative general theory is psychological.[37]

In all his emphasis on actions of man making up the social system, Homans has assumed that the only valid theoretical study of human actions is psychological. By definition he excludes any other approach on the grounds that when a deductive system about any human action or a set of actions is constructed, the major premise always turns out to be a psychological proposition.

Homans illustrates his point by reference to Smelser's study of the development of cotton industry. He says that for all his functionalism, Smelser's actual explanation of innovations in cotton manufacturing can be phrased as follows:

1. Men are more likely to perform an activity, the more valuable they perceive the reward of that activity to be.
2. Men are more likely to perform an activity, the more

successful they perceive the activity is likely to be in getting that reward.

3. The high demand for cotton textiles and the low productivity of labour led men concerned with cotton manufacturing to perceive the development of labour-saving machinery as rewarding in increased profits.

4. The existing state of technology led them to perceive the effort to develop labour-saving machinery as likely to be successful.[38]

In another example Homans tries to explain by means of the same general proposition why William the Conqueror never invaded Scotland. His explanation goes like this:

1. The more rewarding men find the results of an action, the more likely they are to take this action.

2. William the Conqueror was a man.

3. Therefore, the more rewarding William found the results of an action, the more likely he was to take this action.

4. In the given circumstances, he did not find the conquest of Scotland rewarding.

5. Therefore, he was unlikely to take action that would win him Scotland.[39]

It is, however, possible to phrase both arguments in such a way that the major proposition would not be psychological, i.e., would not refer to individual rewards as explaining action, but to group activity. Accordingly, the argument in the first example would go something like this:

1. Specific social conditions create needs for specific types of action.

2. If such needs are present, men are likely to undertake activities which would fulfil these needs.

3. The high demand for cotton textiles and the low productivity of labour was a social need which necessitated some activity by those engaged in cotton manufacturing to meet it.

4. Labour-saving machinery has come to be the type of activity that was successful in meeting this need.

In the second example:

1. The less pressure a group exerts on its members in a given direction, the less likely they are to act in that direction.

2. There was little pressure on William the Conqueror by the group of nobles to conquer Scotland.
3. Therefore, he was unlikely to take action that would win him Scotland.

Stated in this manner both arguments avoid reference to any perception of rewards and their major premises remain sociological. They are deductive in character and their explanatory propositions are of the 'if – then' nature. But these general propositions are not reducible to Homans' general propositions, simply because they state something different. Homans' general propositions explain the specific action as response to reward perception, the latter however, explains it as a response to action of other people. In either case, the focus of determinacy is different.

The trouble with Homans' argument, however, is that it is basically philosophical. It seems that what Homans wants to emphasize is that in reality human actions are ultimately actions of individual human beings, and therefore, the most general proposition concerning any human actions has to be a statement about individual actors. This might be a reasonable metaphysical assumption, but scientific theory does not begin here. Scientific theory begins with analytical abstraction. Thus, when trying to explain the actions of William the Conqueror, one can abstract from his actions the aspects which concern his personality and his personal reward-punishment system, or else one can turn to the aspects which concern his relations with other people of his time. Neither approach is exclusive; on the contrary they are complementary. Either approach can involve true explanatory propositions of a high degree of generality, irreducible to one another, since they deal with two different, albeit interrelated, sets of problems. As is commonly accepted by sociologists, the psychological approach deals with problems which arise in connection with the integration of the actions of an individual actor, who is also a physiological organism, whereas the sociological approach concentrates on problems arising from the social interaction of a plurality of individual actors.[40] In either case, the focus of determinacy is different. Homans is correct in saying that the actions of a man that we take to be evidence of his personality are not different from his actions that, together with the actions of others, make up a social system, they are the same actions. But from this it does not follow that the same set of general propositions are needed for explaining the phenomena of both personality and society. On the contrary, focusing on different aspects of the same phenomena warrants different formal objects for the study of those phenomena and hence different sets of general propositions. As Parsons and Kroeber once stated in reference to anthropology, the analytical distinction between different, although related disciplines, should be consistently maintained and such questions as which discipline is more 'important' or 'fundamental' are not meaningful at all.[41] Indeed, Homans' argument reminds one of the old individual versus society controversy which was so aptly answered by Simmel and Cooley.[42] Not that the question should not be raised again, but any discussion of it should build on previous thinking.

THE EXPLANATORY VALUE OF FUNCTIONALISM

To sum up, contemporary functionalism in sociology, especially as represented by Talcott Parsons, involves two types of causal explanation, (1) what I have called intercausality and (2) what I have called telecausality.

Intercausality means that any variable in the social system can be seen as a true productive cause, provided all the other variables dependent upon it in the system can be assumed to be functioning. At the same time it means that any variable can be a productive cause only in connection with other variables. The value of this approach is that theoretically it is possible to determine the relative causal import of each variable within the system upon the state of the system as a whole. This is what Gouldner has called 'factor weighing'. True, so far functionalist studies have not undertaken such factor weighing. All of them seem to focus on one or two variables, attempting to explain their contribution to the state of the system, but not their contribution to this state relative to one another. Nevertheless, this remains as a next logical step of functional analysis.

If productive causality were to be rejected from functionalism altogether, if the phrase 'contributes to the state of the system' were to have no productively causal meaning at all, then the time element must be taken out of it and it becomes purely static analysis, treating social relations in the abstract only, unable to account for change. Thus, without any productively causal implication, one could say that personal ordering of the countermen by the waitresses is related to a disruptive state of the system, and impersonal ordering is related to an integrating state of the system, but one could never explain why in a concrete restaurant system a change from personal to impersonal ordering should result in a changed state of the system.

Turning now to telecausality and the explanatory value of functionalism deriving from its implications of it, it must be said, first of all, that the question of telecausality in functionalism is a more prominent question than even that of productive causality. The reason for this is that the functionalists, as was already stated, are somehow more concerned with explaining the variables ('items'), or rather their persistence within the system, than simply indicating their 'contribution' to either maintenance or disruption of the system. Typically, in functionalism the latter is used to explain the former.[43] Such telecausal explanation, however, involves no notion of necessity between the state of the system and specific variables within it. Hence the question has been raised whether such explanation is explanation at all. Carl G. Hempel put the problem thus:

> Suppose . . . that we are interested in explaining the occurence of a trait i in a system s (at a certain time t), and that the following functional analysis is offered:

(a) At t, s functions adequately in a setting of kind c (characterized by specific internal and external conditions)

(b) s functions adequately in a setting of kind c only if a certain necessary condition, n, is satisfied.

(c) If trait i were present in s then, as an effect, condition n would be satisfied.

(d) (Hence,) at t, trait i is present in s.

. . . Right now, we will concern ourselves only with the *logic* of the argument; i.e., we will ask whether (d) formally follows from (a), (b), (c), just as in a deductive nomological explanation the explanandum follows from the explanans. The answer is obviously in the negative, for, to put it pedantically, the argument . . . involves the fallacy of affirming the consequent in regard to premise (c). More explicitly, the statement (d) could be validly inferred if (c) asserted that *only* the presence of trait i could effect satisfaction of condition n. As it is, we can infer merely that condition n must be satisfied in some way or other at time t; for otherwise, by reason of (b), the system s could not be functioning adequately in its setting, in contradiction to what (a) asserts. But it might well be that the occurrence of any one of a number of alternative items would suffice no less than the occurrence of i to satisfy requirement n, in which case the account provided by the premises of . . . (the argument) simply fails to explain why trait i rather than one of its alternatives is present in s at t.[44]

Hempel concludes that the explanatory import of functional analysis is rather weak and precarious.

Unfortunately, Hempel misinterprets the object of functional explanation. As was noted previously, functionalism is not concerned with explaining the existence of specific variables, but rather with explaining their *persistence* within a system. Hempel's argument should be stated in different fashion, i.e., his proposition (c) should read 'if trait i were to persist in s, then, as an effect, condition n would be satisfied', and his proposition d should conclude '(Hence,) at t, trait i persists in s'. Now the argument does not try to explain why i, rather than i' or i'' is present within the system, but explains why, granted that i is present in the system, it persists within it. The presence of *i* rather than any other item can be explained in other ways, perhaps historically or anthropologically (e.g., cultural configurationism). Functionalism is not an all-inclusive method that explains everything in society. On the contrary, it complements other approaches and is complemented by them.

Ultimately, the explanatory value of functionalism lies in its holism.[45] Basically this means both explaining the whole in terms of its parts and parts in terms of the whole as the best substitute for the dynamic analysis of which Parsons speaks as the ideal of functionalism. So far, the parts of the whole are conceived by functionalism as structural items affecting in one way or another the state of the whole. Eventually, the parts might be conceived as processes explainable in terms of other processes of the total system. For example, unity of society has been often explained in terms of the authority of the political system. Yet, such argument overlooks the question of what makes political systems possible and assumes that political groups act independently from other social phenomena. Functionalism calls for viewing the political system as a dependent variable. It depends, for one thing, upon the process of institutionalization of norms and values; it has to be seen as dependent upon other subsystems of society, etc. Thus integration of society becomes a question not of any one process but all of them. Each process, however, persists inasmuch as it fulfils a need of the system.

This is the explanatory value of the organismic model assumed by functionalism. All in all, it makes possible explanation of society in terms of its own laws. It enables generalization and thus carries sociology beyond pure historicism, by which all explanation must be relative to specific time and place.[46] No doubt, such position raises some important theoretical problems. A long-standing problem has been that of the individual versus society controversy. Discussion of this problem is beyond the scope of this study.[47] It must be kept in mind, however, that the organicism of functionalism is an analytical theory, not a reified analogy. There are a number of questions connected with this issue which functionalism has yet to study— especially the question of relationship of intended behaviour to societal processes. In what way is the intended purposive behaviour determined by the societal processes? Similarly, emphasis on social processes as cybernetic processes requires more precise study, especially of the telecausality involved in it.

Functionalism's explanatory value derives ultimately from the telecausal implications of its holism. As was explained above, any *tour de force*, aimed at showing that telecausality in functionalism is either a spurious issue or that it can be substituted by other forms of explanation only beclouds the meaning of functionalism. The best procedure to follow is to accept telecausality as part of functional explanatory methodology, and then take it for what it is worth. Rejection of its telecausality makes functionalism a weak theory and a weak methodology. The best approach is to develop its telecausal potentialities and to judge them by the fruitfulness of explanation and research.

It should be kept in mind that the alternative to telecausality is not explanation through productive causes, but explanation by chance. Telecausality explains repetitive and concurrent phenomena. As has been pointed out in the study, productive causality itself can explain occurrence of phenomena, but not the occurrence of their repetition. Repetition thus remains a coincidence, a chance. Explanation by chance, however, is not really an explanation because it gives as much reason for something occurring as it gives for its not occurring. Thus chance could not explain why different processes, many of them conflicting, should persist in producing an equilibrium. Because of its telecausal implication, functionalism is able to explain productively causal phenomena concurring persistently to produce functioning unity of society.

Notes

1. Cf. Richard B. Braithwaite, *Scientific Explanation, A Study of the Function of Theory, Probability and Law in Science* (Cambridge: The University Press, 1953), pp. 1, 9. Also cf. Carl G. Hempel, *Aspects of Scientific Explanation* (New York: The Free Press, 1965), pp. 246–8; Ernest Nagel, *The Structure of Science* (London: Routledge & Kegan Paul, 1961), pp. 29–46; George C. Homans, 'Contemporary Theory in Sociology', *Handbook of Modern Sociology*, ed. Robert E. L. Faris (Chicago: Rand McNally and Co., 1964), p. 951 ff.; Hans L. Zetterberg, *On Theory and Verification in Sociology* (The Bedminster Press, 1965), pp. 96–100, 104 ff.; Paul H. Furfey, *The Scope and Method of Sociology* (New York: Harper and Bros., 1953), pp. 203 ff., 244–58.

2. Cf. Nagel, p. 503 ff.

3. *Ibid.*, p. 511.

4. Cf. *ibid.*, p. 512.

5. Cf. *ibid.*, p. 516.

6. Here middle-range theories are not counterposed to the so-called grand theories. Both types of theories represent an attempt at systematic theory construction. Middle-range theories differ from simple qualitative *ad hoc* hypotheses in that their general propositions are potentially derivable from systematic general theories. For this reason they are able to transcend the time-sample statistical limitations. Thus, Merton's theory of anomie makes sense in as much as it contains such ideas as socialization or institutionalization—paraphernalia of one general theory. The relation between household work and factory work absenteeism can become theoretically significant and transcend *ad hoc* qualitative hypotheses only if some general assumptions are made about expansion of human energy, or about value involvement, or role conflict, or the like.

7. George C. Homans, 'Bringing Men Back In', *American Sociological Review*, 29 (Dec. 1964), pp. 809–18.

8. Cf. Morris R. Cohen, *Reason and Nature* (Glencoe, Ill.: Free Press, 1959), pp. 109–14.

9. Cf. Nagel, pp. 540–6.

10. Cf. Don Martindale, *The Nature and Types of Sociological Theory* (London: Routledge & Kegan Paul, 1960), pp. 285 ff., 339 ff.

11. Cf. Nagel, p. 573.
12. Kingsley Davis, 'The Myth of Functional Analysis as a Special Method in Sociology and Anthropology', *American Sociological Review*, 24 (Dec. 1959), pp. 752–72.
13. Carl G. Hempel, 'The Logic of Functional Analysis', *Symposium on Sociological Theory*, ed. Llewellyn Gross (Evanston, Ill.: Row, Peterson and Co., 1959), pp. 271–307.
14. Cf. Homans, 'Bringing Men Back In'.
15. Cf., for example, Mario Bunge, *Causality, the Place of the Causal Principle in Modern Science* (Cambridge: Harvard University Press, 1959). Also, Braithwaite, *Scientific Explanation*; Nagel, *The Structure of Science;* Hempel, *Aspects of Scientific Explanation*.
16. The only two single works on the subject seem to be Ronald P. Dore, 'Function and Cause', *American Sociological Review*, 26 (Dec. 1961), pp. 843–53, and Henri Janne, 'Function et finalité en sociologie', *Cahiers Internationaux de Sociologie*, 16 (1954), pp. 50–68. Reference to other material is given in the succeeding chapters.
17. Robert M. MacIver, *Social Causation* (New York: Ginn and Co., 1942), pp. 99–100.
18. Bunge, *Causality;* Paul Janet, *Final Causes*, trans. William A. Aleck from second edition (New York: Charles Scribner's and Sons, 1891).
19. Talcott Parsons, *The Social System* (London: Tavistock, 1951), p. 20.
20. Talcott Parsons, *Essays in Sociological Theory*, rev. ed. (Glencoe, Ill.: The Free Press, 1954), pp. 215–16.
21. Robert K. Merton, *Social Theory and Social Structure* (Glencoe, Ill.: The Free Press, 1957), p. 21.
22. Parsons, *Social System*, p. 20.
23. Merton, p. 21.
24. Talcott Parsons, *The Structure of Social Action* (New York: McGraw Hill Book Co., 1937), p. 25 fn.
25. Parsons, *Social System*, p. 21.
26. Parsons, *Essays*, p. 216–17.
27. Parsons, *Social System*, p. 21.
28. Parsons, *Essays*, p. 217.
29. *Ibid.* Parsons, *Social System*, pp. 21–2.
30. Parsons, *Essays*, pp. 217–18.
31. Parsons, *Social System*, pp. 21–2.
32. Cf. Merton, pp. 5–10.
33. *Ibid.*, pp. 46–7.
34. *Ibid.*, p. 26.
35. For a discussion of this difference between Parsons and Merton see Alvin W. Gouldner, 'Reciprocity and Autonomy in Functional Theory', *Symposium on Sociological Theory*, ed. Llewelyn Gross (Evanston, Ill.: Row, Peterson and Co., 1959), pp. 241–70.

36. Merton, p. 55.
37. *Ibid.*, p. 60.
38. *Ibid.*, p. 56.
39. Marion Levy, Jr., *The Structure of Society* (Princeton, N.J.: Princeton University Press, 1952), p. 35, 88.
40. *Ibid.*, p. 36.
41. *Ibid.*, p. 39.
42. *Ibid.*, p. 77.
43. *Ibid.*, pp. 79–80.
44. *Ibid.*, pp. 71–2.
45. *Ibid.*, pp. 88–9.
46. *Ibid.*, pp. 90–6.
47. *Ibid.*, pp. 97–8.
48. Bernard Barber, 'Structural-Functional Analysis: Some Problems and Misunderstandings', *American Sociological Review*, 21 (April 1965), pp. 129–35; Harry C. Bredemeier, 'The Methodology of Functionalism', *American Sociological Review*, 20 (April 1955), pp. 173–80.
49. Barber, pp. 129–35.
50. Bredemeier, pp. 173–80.
51. Bunge, p. 26.
52. Herbert A. Simon, *Models of Man* (New York: John Wiley and Sons, 1957), p. 11.
53. Nicholas S. Timasheff, 'Order, Causality, Conjuncture', *Symposium*, ed. Gross, p. 148.

CHAPTER II

1. Bunge, p. 46.
2. *Ibid.*, p. 41.
3. *Ibid.*, pp. 46–53.
4. Cf. Hempel, pp. 272–5.
5. *Ibid.*, p. 276.
6. Edward C. Devereux, Jr., 'Parsons' Sociological Theory', *The Social Theories of Talcott Parsons*, ed. Max Black (Englewood Cliffs, N.J.: Prentice-Hall, Inc., 1961), p. 56.
7. Cf. Parsons, *Social System*, pp. 180–207.
8. Cf. Devereux, p. 56.
9. Merton, pp. 33–4. Cf. also Parsons, *Social System*, p. 167.
10. Harry M. Johnson, Sociology: *A Systematic Introduction* (London: Routledge & Kegan Paul, 1960), pp. 68–9.
11. *Ibid.*, pp. 69–70.
12. Cf. Merton, pp. 33–6; Johnson, p. 69.
13. Neil Smelser, *Social Change in the Industrial Revolution* (London: Routledge & Kegan Paul, 1959), pp. 71–2.

14. Cf. Parsons, *Essays* (1949 ed.), p. 21.
15. Cf. p. 31 above.
16. MacIver, p. 251.
17. *Ibid.*, pp. 181–4.
18. Talcott Parsons, 'An Outline of the Social System', *Theories of Society*, ed. Talcott Parsons, Edward Shils, Kaspar D. Naegele and Jesse R. Pitts (Glencoe, Ill.: The Free Press, 1961), p. 36.
19. Talcott Parsons and Neil J. Smelser, *Economy and Society* (London: Routledge & Kegan Paul, 1956), p. 79.
20. Cf. Johnson, pp. 56–9, and Parsons and Smelser, pp. 78–85.
21. Gouldner, pp. 264–5.
22. Parsons, *Structure*, p. 576.
23. *Ibid.*, pp. 520–1.
24. Pitirim A. Sorokin, *Contemporary Sociological Theories* (New York and London: Harper and brothers, 1928), p. 690.
25. *Ibid.*, p. 691; also: 'X (Wirtschaftsethik) = f (A [religion]+B+C+ D+E+F . . .) and exacts such and such effects on the economic phenomena. These effects will not only be the effects of A, but B C D E F, . . .' *Ibid.*, cf. also pp. 531-2; And also: 'It is not suffiicent to show that some of the accepted myths, beliefs and dogmas seem to have been "effective". To show their effectiveness, the authors have to take an idea in its pure form and demonstrate with it the accuracy of their theory. Contrariwise, their analysis remains "superficial" and their conclusion unconvincing . . . Since he [Max Weber] takes the religious factor only as a methodological variable, he avoids much of the above objection. Nevertheless, Weber very often slips from his "functional" standpoint into that of one sided "causation". In this case he also makes the above mistake'. *Ibid.*, pp. 689–90.
26. Parsons, *Structure*, p. 632; cf. also pp. 575-8.
27. Cf. Pitirim A. Sorokin, *Sociocultural Casuality, Time, Space* (Durham, N.C.: Duke University Press, 1943), p. 39.

CHAPTER III

1. Parsons, *Essays*, pp. 217–18.
2. Cf. Walter Buckley, 'Structural-Functional Analysis in Modern Sociology', *Modern Sociological Theory in Continuity and Change*, ed. Howard Becker and Alvin Boskoff (New York: The Dryden Press, 1957), p. 246; Dorothy Emmet, *Function, Purpose and Powers* (London: Macmillan and Co., Ltd., 1958), p. 60 ff.; Hempel, pp. 297-9.
3. Nicholas S. Timasheff, *Sociological Theory, Its Nature and Growth*, revised ed. (New York: Random House, 1957), p. 233.
4. Emmet, p. 60.

Notes

5. Harry C. Bredemeier, 'The Methodology of Functionalism', *American Sociological Review*, 20 (April, 1955), pp. 173–80.
6. Johnson, pp. 71–4; cf. also George C. Homans and David M. Schneider, *Marriage, Authority, and Final Causes* (Glencoe, Ill.: The Free Press, 1955).
7. Janne, pp. 50–68.
8. Buckley, p. 246.
9. *Ibid.*, pp. 247–8.
10. Hempel, p. 297–9.
11. Cf. Janet, pp. 17–61.
12. Cf. *ibid.*, p. 25.
13. *Ibid.*, p. 34. Janet follows here J. S. Mill; this is actually the method of concordance.
14. *Ibid.*, p. 40–2.
15. *Ibid.*, p. 61.
16. *Ibid.*, p. 31.
17. *Ibid.*, p. 32.
18. *Ibid.*, p. 51. Here Janet uses a Kantian expression.
19. E. Kant quoted by Janet, *ibid.*, p. 48.
20. The famous dispute as to whether sociology can be a science has derived from the problem of patterns in human history. The idealistic tradition has emphasized the uniqueness of historical forces and hence has made sociology into an analysis or interpretation of history, rather than a generalizing science. Parsons himself holds an indebtedness to this idealistic approach. It seems, however, that today this dispute as to the uniqueness or non-uniqueness of human acts in history is over. Sociologists on one hand have come to admit that not all of human behaviour is patterned, i.e., recurrent or uniform, but on the other hand, they have shown that enough of it is patterned to provide basis for a science. Few of them would take an either-or position anymore. Cf. Parsons, *Structure*, pp. 473–87; Alex Inkeles, *What is Sociology?* (Englewood Cliffs, N.J.: Prentice-Hall, Foundation of Modern Sociology Series, 1964), pp. 93–6; Kurt H. Wolff (ed.), *Emile Durkheim, Essays on Sociology and Philosophy* (New York: Harper Torchbooks, 1964), p. 345 ff; Robin Williams, *American Society, A Sociological Interpretation* (New York: Alfred A. Knopf, 1960), p. 20 ff; Alfred R. Radcliffe-Brown, *Structure and Function in Primitive Society* (London: Cohen & West, 1961), pp. 190–2.
21. Cf. Merton, p. 50.
22. Cf. Marion Levy, Jr., *The Structure of Society* (Princeton, N.J.: Princeton University Press, 1952), pp. 57–8, 64; Merton, p. 50; Parsons, *Social System*, p. 114.
23. Claude Levi-Strauss, 'Social Structure', *Anthropology Today*, prepared by A. L. Kroeber (Chicago: University of Chicago Press, 1953),

p. 525.
24. Levy, pp. 57–8.
25. *Ibid.*, pp. 114–15.
26. Siegfried F. Nadel, *The Theory of Social Structure* (London: Cohen & West, 1957), pp. 149–50.
27. *Ibid.*, pp. 145–6.
28. *Ibid.*, p. 7.
29. Cf. Parsons, *Social System*, p. 34; Parsons, *Theories of Society*, p. 36, 44 ff.
30. Cf. Nadel, p. 150.
31. Cf. Levy, p. 64.
32. *Ibid.*, p. 58.
33. Nadel, p. 128.
34. *Ibid.*, p. 128, 145.
35. *Ibid.*, pp. 145–6.
36. *Ibid.*, p. 128.
37. Cf. *ibid.*, p. 129.
38. Cf. Hempel, p. 278.
39. Parsons, *Social System*, p. 482.
40. Cf. Devereux, p. 34.
41. *Ibid.*, p. 33; cf. also Parsons, *Theories of Society*, p.37.
42. Cf. Parsons, *ibid.*; also Talcott Parsons and Edward A. Shils (eds.) *Toward a General Theory of Action* (Cambridge: Harvard University Press, 1951), pp. 226–7.
43. Cf. Robert Brown, *Explanation in Social Science* (London: Routledge & Kegan Paul, 1963), pp. 110–11; Devereux, p. 53; Ernest Nagel, *Logic Without Metaphysics* (Glencoe, Ill.: The Free Press, 1957), pp. 251–2.
44. Cf. Brown, p. 111.
45. Buckley, pp. 255–6.
46. Nadel, p. 144.
47. Marion Levy, for example, sees social structure as the relation of the various forms of actions to the patterns of the results of action (*Structure*, pp. 60–1). We may add that this relation is achieved by means of the model of equilibrating system by which the results of action are accounted for by the same principle as their productive causes.
48. Nadel, pp. 144–5.
49. Gouldner, pp. 242–3.
50. Cf. *Ibid.*, pp. 243–4.
51. *Ibid.*, pp. 244–5.
52. Cf. Raymond W. Firth, 'Function', *Yearbook of Anthropology, 1955* (New York: Wenner-Gren Foundation for Anthropological Research, 1955), p. 238; Merton, pp. 20–25.
53. This notion of covariance should not be confused with inter-

causality as understood in this study. Intercausality asserts simply that causes act together, not singly, and the effect is a product of this common action. The effect is not seen as a cause. Covariance, or mathematical interdependence, considers the effect to be a cause at the same time so that to designate a variable as either a cause or an effect is actually irrelevant.

54. Cf. George C. Homans, *The Human Group* (Routledge & Kegan Paul, 1950), pp. 110–13. For criticism cf. Paula Brown and Robert Brown, 'A Note on Hypotheses in Homans' *The Human Group*', *American Sociological Review*, 20 (February, 1955), pp. 83–5.

55. Merton, p. 51; also p. 24.

56. *Ibid.*, p. 73, 82.

57. *Ibid.*, p. 52, 80–1.

58. Cf. *ibid.*, p. 27.

59. Ralph Linton, *Study of Man* (New York, London: Appleton-Century-Crofts, 1936), pp. 406–7.

60. Cf. Bronislaw Malinowski, 'Anthropology', *Encyclopedia Britannica*, first supplementary vol., 1926. 13th ed., pp. 131–40.

61. Parsons and Shils, *Toward*, p. 25, 197 ff.

62. Parsons, *Social System*, p. 115.

63. Cf. Talcott Parsons, R. F. Bales, and A. E. Shils, *Working Papers in the Theory of Action* (Glencoe, Ill.: The Free Press, 1953), pp. 64–103; Parsons and Smelser, *Economy*, p. 13 ff; Hempel, pp. 293–7; Nadel, pp. 158–9.

64. Levy, p. 56.

65. *Ibid.*, pp. 87–8.

66. Merton, p. 51.

67. Marion Levy points out that this distinction between the intended but unrecognized functions 'may prove to be useful concepts in treating certain "frustration" phenomena, most notably cases of so-called "compulsive striving." Cf. *Structure*, p. 87.

68. Perhaps the best statement of this 'transformation' of latent functions into manifest is by R. P. Dore: 'Nowadays, with sociologists busily ferreting out latent functions in every nook and cranny of society and their writings gaining general currency, latent functions are not likely to stay latent for long. Here indeed is the complement of the self-fulfilling prophecy—the self-falsifying assertion. The sociologist who contends that X has such and such a latent function in his own society in fact makes that function manifest. The intervention of human purpose to preserve institutions so that they may continue to fulfil their *once* latent functions is likely to occur more frequently as a result.' Dore, p. 845.

69. Cf. Merton, p. 66, 68; also Johnson, p. 68.

70. Several examples of recent research with a functionalist per-

spective are: John Finley Scott, 'The Role of the College Sorority in Endogamy', *American Sociological Review*, 30 (August, 1965), pp. 524-7; James G. Ahler and Joseph B. Tamney, 'Some Functions of the Religious Ritual in a Catastrophe', *Sociological Analysis*, 25 (Winter, 1964), pp. 212-230; Robert A. Ellis and W. Clayton Lane, 'Structural Supports for Upward Mobility', *American Sociological Review*, 28 (October, 1963), pp. 743-56; Herman Turk, 'Social Cohesion Through Variant Values: Evidence from Medical Role Relations', *American Sociological Review*, 28 (February, 1963), pp. 28-37.

CHAPTER IV

1. Parsons and Shils, *Toward*, p. 191.
2. Parsons, *Social System*, pp. 204–5.
3. *Ibid.*, p. 205, 209 ff.
4. *Ibid.*, pp. 206 ff. 297–8.
5. Cf. *ibid.*, pp. 205–6, 298.
6. Cf. *ibid.*, p. 298.
7. The term 'function' could, of course, be used with the technical meaning given to it. But this would hardly eliminate the confusion which derives from the different connotations attached to it.
8. Cf. Chapter III.
9. Parsons, *Social System*, p. 27.
10. *Ibid.*, pp. 29–36.
11. Levy, p. 151.
12. Parsons, *Theories of Society*, p. 38.
13. Parsons and Smelser, *Economy*, p. 16.
14. Parsons, *Theories of Society*, pp. 38–9.
15. *Ibid.*, p. 39.
16. *Ibid.*, p. 40.
17. Cf. Devereaux, p. 114.
18. Parsons, *Theories of Society*, p. 40.
19. Cf. Chapter II.
20. Cf. Chandler Morse, 'The Functional Imperatives', *Social Theories of Talcott Parsons*, ed. Max Black, p. 144.
21. Parsons and Smelser, *Economy*, p. 68; Robert K. Merton, L. Broom, and L. S. Cottrell, Jr., *Sociology Today* (New York: Basic Books, Inc. 1959), p. 17; Morse, p. 128.
22. Parsons and Smelser, *Economy*, p. 68.
23. Cf. Morse, p. 130 ff. For schematic presentations, see Figures 1, 2, and 3 in Appendix I.
24. See tabular presentation in Appendix II.
25. Parsons, *Theories of Society*, p. 64.
26. Cf. *ibid.*, p. 61.

27. Talcott Parsons, 'General Theory in Sociology,' in Merton et al., *Sociology Today*, p. 17.
28. *Ibid.*, p. 18.
29. *Ibid.*, p. 19.
30. Cf. *ibid.*, p. 21.
31. Parsons, *Theories of Society*, p. 66.
32. Cf. *ibid.*, p. 38.
33. *Ibid.*, p. 65.
34. Following N. Wiener, Braithwaite points out that cybernetics is largely concerned with teleological mechanism; Richard B. Braithwaite, *Scientific Explanation, a Study of the Function of Theory, Probability and Law in Science* (Cambridge: The University Press, 1959), p. 328.

CHAPTER V

1. Ernest Nagel, 'Teleological Explanation and Teleological Systems,' *Readings in the Philosophy of Science*, ed. Herbert Feigl and May Brodbeck (New York: Appleton-Century-Crofts, Inc., 1953), pp. 537–58; cf. also Hempel, p. 294.
2. Nagel, 'Teleological Explanation . . .'
3. Cf. for example Dore.
4. Nagel, *Structure of Science*, pp. 404–5.
5. Cf. Harold Fallding, 'Functional Analysis in Sociology', *American Sociological Review*, 28 (February, 1963), pp. 5–13.
6. Cf. Hempel, p. 299; Fallding, pp. 5–13; Carlo L. Lastrucci, *The Scientific Approach* (Cambridge, Mass.: Schenkman Publ. Co., 1963), 185–6; Timasheff, *Sociological Theory*, pp. 232–3.
7. Cf. Merton, *Social Theory*, pp. 23–5, 60 ff; Emmet, p. 97; Lastrucci, p. 185.
8. Alfred J. Ayer, *The Foundations of Empirical Knowledge* (London: Macmillan and Co., Ltd., 1955), p. 183.
9. *Ibid.*, pp. 185–6.
10. *Ibid.*, p. 199.
11. Morris R. Cohen and Ernest Nagel, *An Introduction to Logic and Scientific Method* (London: Kegan Paul, 1934), pp. 266–7.
12. *Ibid.*, p. 271; Lastrucci, pp. 186–88.
13. Braithwaite, pp. 302–3; cf. also Hempel, p. 276.
14. Cohen and Nagel, p. 273.
15. Cf. Parsons, *Theories of Society*, p. 37.
16. Fallding, p. 7.
17. 'If a precise hypothesis of self-regulation for systems of a specified kind is set forth, then it becomes possible to explain, and to predict categorically, the satisfaction of certain functional requirements simply on the basis of information concerning antecedent needs; and the

hypothesis can then be objectively tested by an empirical check of its predictions.' Hempel, p. 290.

18. Cf. Merton, *Social Theory*, p. 51.

19. Paul Hanly Furfey, *The Scope and Method of Sociology* (New York: Harper and Brothers, 1953), pp. 102–3.

20. Paul H. Furfey summarizes the physicalist position of the Vienna Circle thus: 'Physicalism demands that all sciences, including the social sciences, should speak a common language and that this common language should be the language of physics. Thus all science is, in a sense, reduced to physics. This does not necessarily mean that the language of all sciences will remain mechanistic; this will be the case as long as physics itself is expressed mechanistically; but if physics changes its mode of expression, the other sciences will follow suit. Physicalism demands that all sociological statements be reduced to statements of arrangements in time and space.' Furfey, p. 40; cf. also Victor Kraft, *The Vienna Circle* (New York: Philosophical Library, 1953).

21. A notable exception is R. B. Braithwaite. Chapter X of his *Scientific Explanation* presents an attempt to establish teleology as an independent form of scientific explanation.

22. Cf. Emmet, pp. 45–70. For some contemporary works on teleology cf. D. M. Allan, 'Towards a Natural Teleology', *Journal of Philosophy*, 49 (June 19, 1952), pp. 449–59; E. E. Harris, 'Teleology and Teleological Explanation', *Journal of Philosophy*, 56 (January 1, 1959), pp. 5–25; R. Hansmann, 'Mechanism or Teleology in the Creative Process', *Journal of Philosophy*, 58 (September 28, 1961), pp. 577–84; A Hofstadter, 'Objective Teleology', *Journal of Philosophy*, 38 (January 16, 1941), pp. 29–39; A. Rosenblueth, 'Behaviour, Purpose and Teleology', *Philosophy of Science*, 10 (January, 1943) pp. 18–24; C. H. Waddington, 'True and False Teleology', *Nature*, 145 (May 4, 1940), p. 705.

23. Kingsley Davis, 'The Myth of Functional Analysis as a Special Method in Sociology and Anthropology', *American Sociological Review*, 24 (December, 1959), p. 759.

24. For other criticism of Davis' position, cf. Don Martindale, *The Nature and Types of Sociological Theory* (Boston: Houghton Mifflin Co., 1960), p. 446 ff.

25. Cf. Furfey, pp. 199–200; Lastrucci, pp. 35–6.

26. F. S. C. Northrop talks also about 'concepts by postulation', which in his definition are concepts whose meaning derives from the postulates of a specific theory in which they occur. Cf. *The Logic of the Sciences and the Humanities* (New York: Meridian Books, Inc., 1959), p. 83.

27. Cf. Furfey, p. 244 ff; Cohen and Nagel, p. 197 ff.

28. May Brodbeck, 'Models, Meaning, and Theories,' *Symposium*, ed.

Gross, p. 379.

29. Cf. Merton, *Social Theory*, p. 25 ff; Hempel, p. 290; Levy, p. 29 ff.

30. Cf. Hempel, p. 301. On the postulation of this proposition of integration by Talcott Parsons, cf. his *Social System*, p. 19.

31. Merton, *Social Theory*, pp. 27–8.

32. Davis, p. 764; Dore, p. 846.

33. J. H. M. Beattie, 'Contemporary Trends in British Social Anthropology', *Sociologus*, 1955, pp. 6–7, cited in Werner Stark, *The Fundamental Forms of Social Thought* (London: Routledge & Kegan Paul, 1963), p. 98.

34. Cf. Merton, *Social Theory*, p. 25 ff.

35. Cf. Dore, pp. 851–2.

36. George C. Homans, 'Bringing Men Back In', *American Sociological Review*, V. 29 (December, 1964), pp. 809–18.

37. George C. Homans, 'Contemporary Theory in Sociology', *Handbook of Modern Sociology*, ed. Robert E. L. Faris (Chicago: Rand McNally and Co., 1964), p. 970.

38. Homans, 'Bringing Men Back In'.

39. Homans, *Handbook*, p. 968.

40. Cf. Parsons *et al*, *Toward a General Theory of Action*, p. 7.

41. Cf. A. L. Kroeber and T. Parsons, 'The Concepts of Culture and of Social System', *American Sociological Review*, V. 23 (October, 1958), p. 582.

42. Cf. Georg Simmel, *The Sociology of Georg Simmel*, translated and edited by Kurt H. Wolff (Glencoe, Ill.: The Free Press, 1950), pp. 4–6; Charles H. Cooley, *Human Nature and the Social Order*, rev. edition, 1922, pp. 36–7.

43. Cf. Hempel, pp. 282–3.

44. *Ibid.*, pp. 283–4.

45. Don Martindale, 'Limits and Alternatives to Functionalism in Sociology', *Functionalism in the Social Sciences*, ed. Martindale, pp. 154–5.

46. Cf. Chapter II above; also Parsons, *Structure*, pp. 473–87. On the problem of historicism as a background for development of sociology cf. Carlo Antoni, *From History to Sociology* (Detroit: Wayne State University Press, 1959).

47. For a recent discussion of the individual versus society controversy, cf. Werner Stark, *Fundamental Forms of Social Thought*.

Appendix I

The following figures are taken from *Economy and Society*
by Talcott Parsons and Neil J. Smelser, pp. 71, 77, 79.

Figure 1

THE DOUBLE INTERCHANGE BETWEEN THE ECONOMY
AND THE PATTERN-MAINTENANCE SUB-SYSTEM

A_G (*Adaptation*) L_G (*Latency*)
'Economic' Decisions   'Household' Decisions

Labour Services

Decision to   Decision to accept
offer employment   Wages   employment

Consumer Spending

Consumer Goods

Decision to produce   Decision to purchase

and Services

Figure 2

THE DOUBLE INTERCHANGE BETWEEN THE
ECONOMY AND THE POLITY

A_A (*Adaptation*) G_A (*Goal-Attainment*)
'Economic' Decisions   'Political' Decisions

Control over
Capital Funds

Decisions to borrow or   Decision to supply
otherwise obtain liquid   liquid resources through
resources   creation of capital funds

Rights to Intervene

Encouragement of
Productive Enterprise

Decisions to capitalize or   Decision to encourage or
otherwise enhance productive   discourage enterprise
capacity

Control of Productivity

Appendix I

Figure 3

A_I (*Adaptation*) I (*Integration*)
'Economic' Decisions   'Integrative' Decisions

Entrepreneurial Service

$\longleftarrow$————————

Decision to offer oppor-   Decision to offer integ
tunity to entrepreneurs   rative services to the
                                                     economy

Profit

————————$\longrightarrow$

Demand for new

$\longleftarrow$————————

product combinations

Decision to Innovate   Decision to change con
                                                     sumption patterns

New output combinations

————————$\longrightarrow$

Appendix II

Schematic Tabulation of Societal Inputs and Outputs,
from Parsons *et al., Theories of Society,* p. 61.

Primary Social Subsystem	Input and Source	Output and Destination
Pattern-Maintenance	Given structure as institutionalized patterns of normative culture (no external source)	Maintenance of structure and specification of values (no external destination)
Integration	Plasticity (from behavioral organism)	Patterns for purposive response (to behavioral organism)
Goal-Attainment	Capacity for socialized motivational commitments (from personality)	Goal-gratification (to personality)
Adaptation	Codes for organization of information (from cultural system)	Validation of standards of competence (to cultural system)

Bibliography

BOOKS

ANSCOMBE, GERTRUDE E.M. *Intention*. Ithaca, N.Y.: Cornell University Press, 1957.

ANTONI, CARLO. *From History to Sociology*. Detroit: Wayne State University Press, 1959.

ARGYLE, MICHAEL. *The Scientific Study of Social Behaviour*. London: Methuen, 1957.

ARROW, KENNETH J. (ed). *Stanford Symposium on Mathematical Models in the Social Sciences*. Stanford, Calif.: Stanford University Press, 1959.

AYER, ALFRED J. *The Foundations of Empirical Knowledge*. London: Macmillan and Co., Ltd., 1955.

BATESON, GREGORY. *Naven*. 2nd ed. Stanford, Calif.: Stanford University Press, 1958.

BECKER, HOWARD and BOSKOFF, ALVIN (eds.). *Modern Sociological Theory in Continuity and Change*. New York: The Dryden Press, 1957.

BECKWITH, BURNHAM P. *Religion, Philosophy and Science: An Introduction to Logical Positivism*. New York: Philosophical Library, 1957.

BELLAH, ROBERT N. *Tokugawa Religion*. Glencoe, Ill.: The Free Press, 1957.

BLACK, MAX (ed.). *The Social Theories of Talcott Parsons*. Englewood Cliffs, N.J.: Prentice-Hall, Inc., 1961.

BLAU, PETER M. *The Dynamics of Bureaucracy*. Chicago: University of Chicago Press, 1955.

BRAITHWAITE, RICHARD B. *Scientific Explanation, a Study of the Function of Theory, Probability and Law in Science*. Cambridge: The University Press, 1953.

BRAYBROOKE, DAVID (ed.). *Philosophical Problems of the Social Sciences*. New York, London: Macmillan and Co., Ltd., Sources in Philosophy Series, 1965.

BROWN, ROBERT. *Explanation in Social Science*. London: Routledge & Kegan Paul, 1963.

BUNGE, MARIO. *Causality, the Place of the Causal Principle in Modern Science*. Cambridge: Harvard Univeristy Press, 1959.

CASSIRER, ERNEST. *Essay on Man*. New Haven: Yale University Press, 1944.

COHEN, MORRIS R. and NAGEL, ERNEST. *An Introduction to Logic and Scientific Method*. London: Kegan Paul, 1934.

Bibliography

COSER, LEWIS A. *The Function of Social Conflict*. London: Routledge & Kegan Paul, 1956.

D'ABRO, A. *The Decline of Mechanism in Modern Physics*. New York: Van Norstrand, 1939.

— *The Rise of the New Physics*. New York: Dover Publications, 1951.

EMMET, DOROTHY. *Function, Purpose and Powers: Some Concepts in the Study of Individuals and Societies*. London: Macmillan and Co., Ltd., 1958.

FEIGL, HERBERT and BRODBECK, MAY. (eds.). *Readings in the Philosophy of Science*. New York: Appleton-Century-Crofts, Inc., 1953.

FIRTH, RAYMOND W. *Elements of Social Organization*. London: Watts, 1951.

FRANCIS, ROY G. *The Rhetoric of Science*. Minneapolis: University of Minneapolis Press, 1961.

FRANK, PHILLIP. *The Validation of Scientific Theories*. Boston: Beacon Press, 1956

FURFEY, PAUL H. *The Scope and Method of Sociology*. New York: Harper and Bros., 1953.

GIBSON, QUENTIN. *The Logic of Social Enquiry*. London: Routledge & Kegan Paul, 1960.

GLUCKMAN, MAX. *Rituals of Rebellion in South-East Africa*. Manchester: University of Manchester Press, 1954.

GROSS, LLEWELLYN (ed.). *Symposium of Sociological Theory*. Evanston, Ill.: Row, Peterson and Co., 1959.

HOBSON, JOHN A. *Free Thought in the Social Sciences*. London: George Allen and Unwin, 1926.

HOMANS, GEORGE C. *The Human Group*. London: Routledge & Kegan Paul, 1950.

— and SCHNEIDER, DAVID M. *Marriage, Authority, and Final Causes*. Glencoe, Ill.: The Free Press, 1955.

INKELES, ALEX. *What is Sociology?* Englewood Cliffs, N. J.: Prentice-Hall, Foundations of Modern Sociology Series, 1964.

JANET, PAUL. *Final Causes*. trans. from 2nd ed. by WILLIAM ALECK. New York: Charles Scribner's Sons, 1891.

JOHNSON, HARRY M. *Sociology: A Systematic Introduction*. London: Routledge & Kegan Paul, 1960.

KAPLAN, ABRAHAM. *The Conduct of Inquiry, Methodology for Behavioral Sciences*. San Francisco: Chandler Publishing Co., 1964.

KAUFMANN, FELIX. *Methodology of the Social Sciences*. New York: The Humanities Press, 1958.

KRAFT, VICTOR. *The Vienna Circle*. New York: Philosophical Library, 1953.

KROEBER, A. L. (comp.). *Anthropology Today*. Chicago: University of Chicago Press, 1953.

LANDHEER, BARTHOLOMEW. *Mind and Society*. Nijhoff: The Hague, 1952.

LASTRUCCI, CARLO L. *The Scientific Approach*. Cambridge, Mass.: Schenkman Publishing Co., 1963.

LENZEN, VICTOR F. *Causality in Natural Science*. Springfield, Ill.: Thomas Publishing Co., 1954.

LERNER, DANIEL and LASSWELL, HAROLD D. *The Policy Sciences*. Stanford, Calif.: Stanford University Press, 1951.

LEVY, MARION, JR. *The Structure of Society*. Princeton, N. J.: Princeton University Press, 1952.

LINTON, RALPH. *Study of Man*. New York, London: Appleton-Century-Crofts, 1936.

MCEWEN, WILLIAM P. *The Problem of Social-Scientific Knowledge*. Totowa, N.J.: The Bedminster Press, 1963.

MACIVER, ROBERT M. *Social Causation*. New York: Ginn and Co., 1942.

MALINOWSKI, BRONISLAW. *A Scientific Theory of Culture and Other Essays*. New York: Oxford University Press, 1960.

MANNHEIM, ERNEST and KECSKEMETI, PAUL (eds.). *Essays on the Sociology of Culture*. London: Routledge and Kegan Paul, 1956.

MARTINDALE, DON (ed.). *Functionalism in the Social Sciences*. Monograph 5 in a series sponsored by the American Academy of Political and Social Sciences, Philadelphia: American Academy of Political and Social Sciences, February, 1965.

— *The Nature and Types of Sociological Theory*. London: Routledge & Kegan Paul, 1960.

MERTON, ROBERT K. *Social Theory and Social Structure*. Glencoe, Ill.: The Free Press, 1957.

— BROWN, L. and COTTRELL, L. S., JR. *Sociology Today*. New York: Basic Books, Inc., 1959.

— and NISBET, R. A. (eds.). *Contemporary Social Problems*. New York: Harcourt, Brace, 1961.

NADEL, SIEGFRIED F. *The Theory of Social Structure*. London: Cohen & West, 1957.

NAGEL, ERNEST. *Logic Without Metaphysics*. Glencoe, Ill.: The Free Press, 1956.

— *Sovereign Reason*. Glencoe, Ill.: The Free Press, 1954.

NATANSON, MAURICE. *Philosophy of the Social Sciences, A Reader*. New York: Random House, 1963.

NORTHROP, FILMER S. C. *The Logic of the Sciences and the Humanities*. New York: Meridian Books, Inc., 1959.

PARSONS, TALCOTT. *Essays in Sociological Theory*. Revised ed. Glencoe Ill.: The Free Press, 1954.

— *The Social System*. London: Tavistock, 1951.

— *Structure and Process in Modern Societies*. Glencoe, Ill.: The Free Press, 1960.

Bibliography

PARSONS, TALCOTT. *The Structure of Social Action*. New York: McGraw Hill Book Co., Inc., 1937.

— BALES, R. F., OLDS, J. *et. al. Family Socialization and Interaction Process*. London: Routledge & Kegan Paul, 1955.

— and SHILS, EDWARD A. (eds.). *Toward a General Theory of Action*. Cambridge: Harvard University Press, 1951.

— SHILS, E. A., and BALES, R. F. *Working Papers in the Theory of Action*. Glencoe, Ill.: The Free Press, 1953.

— SHILS, E., NAEGELE, K. and PITTS, J. S. (eds.) *Theories of Society*. Vol. I and II. Glencoe Ill.: The Free Press, 1961.

— and SMELSER, NEIL J. *Economy and Society*. London: Routledge & Kegan Paul, 1956.

POPPER, KARL R. *The Logic of Scientific Discovery*. London: Hutchison, 1960.

RADCLIFFE-BROWN, ALFRED R. *Structure and Function in Primitive Society*. London: Cohen & West, 1961.

REISER, OLIVER L. *The Integration of Human Knowledge*. Boston: P. Sargent, 1958.

REX, JOHN. *Key Problems of Sociological Theory*. London: Routledge & Kegan Paul, 1961.

SIMON, HERBERT A. *Models of Man*. New York: John Wiley and Sons, Inc., 1957.

SMELSER, NEIL J. *Social Change in the Industrial Revolution*. London: Routledge & Kegan Paul, 1959.

SMITH, FREDERICK V. *Explanation of Human Behaviour*. London: Constable and Co., Ltd., 1960.

SOROKIN, PITIRIM A. *Contemporary Sociological Theories*. New York and London: Harper and brothers, 1928.

— *Fads and Foibles in Modern Sociology and Related Sciences*. Chicago: Henry Ragnay Co., 1956.

— *Sociocultural Causality ,Time, Space*. Durham, N.C.: Duke University Press, 1943.

STARK, WERNER. *The Fundamental Forms of Social Thought*. London: Routledge & Kegan Paul, 1963.

STEBBING, L. SUSAN. *A Modern Introduction to Logic*. London: Methuen, 1950.

STEWARD, JULIAN H. *Theory of Culture Change*. Urbana, Ill.: University of Illinois Press, 1955.

TIMASHEFF, NICHOLAS S. *Sociological Theory, Its Nature and Growth*. Revised ed. New York: Random House, 1957.

VAN MELSEN, ANDREW G. *The Philosophy of Nature*. 2nd ed.; Duquesne Studies, Philosophical Series No. 2. Pittsburgh, Pa.: Duquesne University Press, 1954.

WHYTE, WILLIAM F. *Human Relations in the Restaurant Industry*. New York: Mcgraw Hill Book Co., 1948.

Bibliography

WIENER, NORBERT. *Cybernetics*. 2nd ed. Cambridge Mass.: M.I.T. Press, 1961.
— *The Human Use of Human Beings*. Boston: Houghton, 1950.
WILLIAMS, ROBIN M. *American Society, A Sociological Interpretation*. New York: Alfred A. Knopf, 1960.
WOLFF, KURT H. (ed.) *Emile Durkheim, Essays on Sociology and Philosophy*. New York: Harper Torchbooks, 1964.

ARTICLES AND PERIODICALS

ABERLE, D. F., COHEN, A. R., *et al.* 'The Functional Prerequisites of a Society', *Ethics*, 60 (January, 1950), pp. 100–11.
AHLER, JAMES G. and TAMNEY, JOSEPH B. 'Some Functions of the Religious Ritual in a Catastrophe', *Sociological Analysis*, 25 (Winter, 1964), pp. 212–30.
ALLAN, D. MAURICE. 'Towards a Natural Teleology', *Journal of Philosophy*, 49 (June 19, 1952), pp. 449–59.
ALLEN, G. O. 'Causal Structure of Value', *Journal of Philosophy*, 56 (March 26, 1959), pp. 327–33.
ANDERSON, A. R. 'Causation in Society', *Review of Metaphysics*, 16 (September, 1962), pp. 62–7.
BAERWALD, FRIEDRICH. 'Society as a Process', *American Catholic Sociological Review*, 5 (December, 1944), pp. 238–43.
BAGBY, R. H. 'Culture and the Causes of Culture', *American Anthropologist*, 55 (October, 1953), pp. 535–54.
Replies with Rejoinder: R. A. MANNERS; J. BEATTIE, 56 (June, 1954), pp. 446–56.
BARBER, BERNARD. 'Structural-Functional Analysis: Some Problems and Misunderstandings', *American Sociological Review*, 21 (April, 1956), pp. 129–35.
BERNARD, F. M. 'Herfer's Treatment of Causation and Continuity in History', *Journal of the History of Ideas*, 24 (April, 1963), pp. 197–212.
BECKER, A. P. 'Some Philosophical Aspects of Economics', *Philosophy of Science*, 15 (July, 1948), pp. 242–6.
BECKER, HOWARD. 'The Nature and Consequences of Black Propaganda', *American Sociological Review*, 14 (April, 1949), pp. 221–35.
BELL, C. G. 'Mechanistic Replacement of Purpose in Biology', *Philosophy of Science*, 15 (January, 1948), pp. 47–51.
BIERSTEDT, ROBERT. 'The Logico-Meaningful Method of P. A. Sorokin', *American Sociological Review*, 2 (December, 1937), pp. 13–23.
— 'The Means-End Scheme in Sociological Theory', *American Sociological Review*, 3 (October, 1938), pp. 665–71.
BOSKOFF, ALVIN. 'Structure, Function and Folk Society', *American Sociological Review*, 14 (December, 1949), pp. 749–58.
BREDEMEIER, HARRY C. 'The Methodology of Functionalism', *American Sociological Review*, 20 (April, 1955). pp. 173–80.

Bibliography

BROWN, PAULA and BROWN, ROBERT. 'A Note on Hypotheses in Homan's *The Human Group*', *American Sociological Reviwe*, 20 (February, 1955), pp. 83–5.

BUCKLEY, WALTER. 'Social Stratification and the Functional Theory of Social Differentiation', *American Sociological Review*, 23 (August, 1958), pp. 369–75.

BURKS, A. W. 'Logic of Causal Propositions', *Mind*, 60 (July, 1951), pp. 363–82.

CAUCIN, FRANCESCA. 'Functional Analysis of Change', *American Sociological Review*, 25 (December, 1960), pp. 818–27.

COUBLORN, R. 'Causes in Culture', *American Anthropologist*, 54 (June, 1952), pp. 112–16.

DAHRENDORF, RALPH. 'Out of Utopia', *American Journal of Sociology*, 64 (September, 1958), pp. 115–27.

DAVIS, KINGSLEY. 'The Myth of Functional Analysis as a Special Method in Sociology and Anthropology', *American Sociological Review*, 24 (December, 1959), 752–72.

— and MOORE, WILBERT. 'Some Principles of Stratification', *American Sociological Review*, 10 (April, 1945), pp. 242–49.

DORE, RONALD P. 'Function and Cause', *American Sociological Review*, 26 (December, 1961), pp. 843–53.

DUBIN, ROBERT. 'Parsons' Actor: Continuities in Social Theory', *American Sociological Review*, 25 (August, 1960), pp. 457–66.

DUCASSE, C. J. 'On the Analysis of Causality,' *Journal of Philosophy*, 54 (June 20, 1957), pp. 422–6.

ELLIOTT, W. F. 'Note on Cause and Effect: Non-Teleological Theory of Causation,' *Pacific Spectator*, 3 (1949), pp. 284–8.

ELLIS, ROBERT A. and LANE, W. CLAYTON. 'Structural Supports for Upward Mobility', *American Sociological Review*, 28 (October, 1963), pp. 743–56.

FALES, W. 'Causes and Effects', *Philosophy of Science*, 20 (January, 1953), pp. 67–74.

FALK, W. D. 'Action-Guiding Reasons', *Journal of Philosophy*, 60 (November 7, 1963), pp. 702–18.

FALLDING, HAROLD. 'Functional Analysis in Sociology', *American Sociological Review*, 28 (February, 1963), pp. 5–13.

FEUER, L. S. 'Causality in the Social Sciences', *Journal of Philosophy*, 51 (November 11, 1954), pp. 681–706.

FEYERABENDT, R. K. 'Metascience', *Philosophical Review*, 70 (July, 1961), pp. 396–405.

FIRTH, RAYMOND W. 'Function', *Yearbook of Anthropology, 1955*. New York: Wenner-Gren Foundation for Anthropological Research, 1955, pp. 237–58.

FOOTE, NELSON N. 'Identification as the Basis for a Theory of Motivation', *American Sociological Review*, 16 (February, 1951), pp. 14–21.

FRIES, H. S. 'Science, Causation and Value', *Philosophy of Science*, 14 (July, 1947), pp. 179–80.

GEIGER, T. 'Human Society and Scientific Laws', *Canadian Journal of Economics and Political Science*, 18 (May, 1952), pp. 184–94.

GINSBERG, MORRIS. 'Social Change', *British Journal of Sociology*, 9 (September, 1958), pp. 220–8.

GOLD, D. 'Independent Causation in Multivariate Analysis: The Case of Political Alienation and Attitude Toward a School Bond Issue', *American Sociological Review*, 27 (February, 1962), pp. 85–7.

GOLDENWEISER, ALEXANDER. 'The Concept of Causality in the Physical and Social Sciences', *American Sociological Review*, 3 (October, 1938), pp. 624–36.

GOLDING, M. P. 'Causation in the Law', *Journal of Philosophy*, 59 (February 15, 1962), pp. 85-95.

GOLDSTEIN, LEON J. 'The Logic of Explanation in Malinowskian Anthropology', *Philosophy of Science*, 24 (April, 1957), pp. 156–66.

GOODE, WILLIAM J. 'Structure and Function: Four Overlapping Conceptual Sets', *Social Review*, 42 (September, 1950), pp. 171–8.

GOTTSCHALK, D. W. 'Causality and Emergence', *Philosophical Review*, 51 (July, 1942). pp. 397–405.

GROSS, EDWARD. 'Some Functional Consequences of Primary Controls in Formal Work Organizations', *American Sociological Review*, 18 (August, 1953), pp. 368–73.

HALLOWELL, A. I. 'The Social Function of Anxiety in a Primitive Society', *American Sociological Review*, 6 (December, 1941), pp. 869–81.

HANCOCK, R. 'Interpersonal and Physical Causation', *Philosophical Review*, 71 (July, 1962), pp. 369–76.

HARRIS, ERROL E. 'Teleology and Teleological Explanation', *Journal of Philosophy*, 56 (January 1, 1959), pp. 5–25.

HAUSMAN, CARL R. 'Mechanism or Teleology in the Creative Process', *Journal of Philosophy*, 58 (September 28, 1961), pp. 577–84.

HEIDER, F. 'Social Perception and Phenomenal Causality', *Psychological Review*, 21 (July, 1946), pp. 3-23.

HEMPEL, CARL G. 'Studies in the Logic of Explanation', *Philosophy of Science*, 15 (April, 1948), pp. 135-75.

HERRMANN, H. 'Account of Recent Biological Methodology: Causal Law and Transplanar Analysis', *Philosophy of Science*, 20 (April, 1953), pp. 149–56.

HOFSTADTER, A. 'Causal Universe', *Journal of Philosophy*, 46 (August 4, 1949), pp. 485–96.

— 'Objective Teleology', *Journal of Philosophy*, 38 (January 16, 1941), pp. 29–39.

Bibliography

HULETT, J. E. JR. 'Estimating the Net Effect of a Commercial Motion Picture Upon the Trend of Local Public Opinion', *American Sociological Review*, 14 (April, 1949), pp. 263–75.

JACOBSON, M. 'Causality and Time in Poetical Process: A Speculation', *American Political Science Review*, 58 (March, 1964), pp. 15–22.

JANNE, HENRI. 'Function et finalité en sociologie', *Cahiers Internationaux de Sociologie*, 16 (Année, 1954), pp. 50–68.

JONAS, H. 'Critique of Cybernetics', *Social Research*, 20 (July, 1953), pp. 172–92.

JONASSEN, KRISTEN. 'The Protestant Ethic and the Spirit of Capitalism in Norway', *American Sociological Review*, 12 (December, 1947), pp. 676–86.

KELSEN, H. 'Causality and Retribution in the Evolution of Human Thought', *Philosophy of Science*, 8 (October, 1941), pp. 533–66.

— 'Causality and Imputation', *Ethics*, 61 (October, 1950), pp. 1–11.

— 'Society and Nature: A Sociological Inquiry', *Review Isis*, 36 (1946), pp. 142–6.

KOMAROVSKY, MIRRA. 'Functional Analysis of Sex Roles', *American Sociological Review*, 15 (August, 1950), pp. 508–16.

KRIKORIAN, Y. H. 'H. J. Allen Singer on Mechanism and Teleology', *Journal of Philosophy*, 54 (September 12, 1957), pp. 569–76.

— 'Life, Mechanism and Purpose', *Philosophy of Science*, 10 (July, 1943), pp. 184–90.

KSHIRSAGER, A. M. 'Prediction from Simultaneous Equation Systems and Wold's Implicit Causal Chain Model', *Econometrica*, 30 (October, 1962), pp. 801–11.

LACKS, J. 'Epiphenominalism and the Notion of Cause', *Journal of Philosophy*, 60 (March 14, 1963), pp. 141–6.

LAWRENCE, N. 'Causality: Causes as Classes', *Review of Metaphysics*, 12 (December, 1958), pp. 161–85.

LEBERGOTT, S. 'Chance and Circumstance: Are Laws of History Possible?' *Journal of Philosophy*, 61 (July 20, 1944), pp. 393–411.

LEVINE, SAUL M. and DORNBLUM, ARTHUR. 'The Implications of Science as a Logical System', *American Sociological Review*, 4 (June, 1939), pp. 381–7.

LOCKWOOD, DAVID. 'Some Remarks on the "Social System",' *British Journal of Sociology*, 7 (June, 1956), pp. 134–45.

LONDON, I. D. 'Some Consequences for History and Psychology of Longuir's Concept of Convergence and Divergence of Phenomena', *Psychological Review*, 53 (May, 1946), pp. 170–88.

LUNDBERG, GEORGE A. 'Contemporary Positivism in Sociology', *American Sociological Review*, 4 (February, 1939), pp. 42–55.

MCCORMICK, THOMAS C. 'Toward Causal Analysis in the Prediction of Attributes', *American Sociological Review*, 17 (February, 1952), pp. 35–44.

Bibliography

MALINOWSKI, BRONISLAW. 'Anthropology', *Encyclopedia Britannica*, first supplementary vol. to the 13th ed., 1926, pp. 131–40.

MENEFEE, SELDEN C. 'The effect of Stereotyped Words on Political Judgements', *American Sociological Review*, 1 (August, 1936), p. 614.

MERTON, ROBERT K. 'The Unanticipated Consequences of Purposive Social Action', *American Sociological Review*, 1 (December, 1936), pp. 894–904.

MILLER, D. S. 'Events in Modern Philosophy: Hume's Analysis of the Relation of Cause to Effect', *Philosophical Review*, 54 (November, 1945), pp. 593–606.

NADEL, SIEGFRIED F. 'Social Control and Self-Regulation', *Social Forces*, 31 (March, 1953), pp. 265–73.

NOWAK, S. 'Some Problems of Causal Interpretation of Statistical Relationships', *Philosophy of Science*, 27 (January, 1960), pp. 23–38.

OLIVER, W. D. 'Logic and Necessity', *Journal of Philosophy*, 47 (February, 1960), pp. 69–73.

PAP, A. 'Note on Causation and the Meaning of Event', *Journal of Philosophy*, 54 (March 14, 1957), pp. 155–9.

PARSONS, TALCOTT. 'Pattern Variables Revisited', *American Sociological Review*, 25 (August, 1960), pp. 467–83.

PHILLIPS, H. L. 'Causation and Selectivity', *Philosophy of Science*, 9 (April, 1942), pp. 139–45

RIESER, M. 'Methodological Investigation into the General Law of Causality', *Journal of Philosophy*, 45 (November 18, 1948), pp. 655–62.

RIKER, W. H. 'Causes of Events', *Journal of Philosophy*, 55 (March 27, 1958), pp. 281–91.

ROSENBLUETH, ARTURO, WIENER, NORBERT and BIGELOW, JULIAN. 'Behavior, Purpose and Teleology', *Philosophy of Science*, 10 (January, 1943), pp. 18–24.

SCHLEGEL, R. 'Mario Bunge on Causality', *Philosophy of Science*, 28 (January, 1961), pp. 72–82. Reply: M. BUNGE, 29 (July, 1962), pp. 306–17.

SCHWARTZ, RICHARD D. 'Functional Alternatives to Inequality', *American Sociological Review*, 24 (December, 1959), pp. 772–82.

SCOTT, JOHN F. 'The Role of the College Sorority in Endogamy', *American Sociological Review*, 30 (August, 1965), pp. 514–27.

SELLARS, W. 'Causation and Perception: An Exploration of the Possibilities of a Realistic Empiricism', *Philosophical Review*, 53 (November, 1944), pp. 534–56.

— 'Positivism in Contemporary Philosophic Thought', *American Sociological Review*, 4 (February, 1939), pp. 26–42.

SELZNICK, PHILLIP. 'Natural Law and Sociology', *Natural Law Forum*, 6 (1961), pp. 84–108.

Bibliography

SIMPSON, RICHARD L. 'A Modification of the Functional Theory of Stratification', *Social Forces*, 35 (December, 1956), pp. 132–7.

SPARSHOTT, F. E. 'Concept of Purpose', *Ethics*, 72 (April, 1962), pp. 157–70.

SPEIRE, HANS. 'Class Structure and "Total War",' *American Sociological Review*, 4 (June, 1939), pp. 370–80.

STEWARD, J. H. 'Culture, Causality and Law: A Trial Formulation of the Development of Early Civilization', *American Anthropologist*, 51 (January, 1949), pp. 1–27. Reply: WATSON, J. E., 51 (July, 1949), pp. 528–9.

— 'Levels of Sociocultural Integration', *Southwestern Journal of Anthropology*, 7 (Winter, 1951), pp. 374–90.

SWANSON, G. E. 'The Approach to a General Theory of Action by Parsons and Shils', *American Sociological Review*, 18 (April, 1953), pp. 125–34.

TAPP, E. J. 'Some Aspects of Causation in History', *Journal of Philosophy*, 49 (January 31, 1952), pp. 69–79.

TASCHDJIAN, E. 'Some Remarks Regarding the Extensional and Intensional Concept of Sociological Variables and Functions', *Chinese Social and Political Science Review*, 24 (April, 1940), pp. 5–14.

TROYER, WILLIAM L. 'Mead's Social and Functional Theory of Mind', *American Sociological Review*, 11 (April, 1946), pp. 198–202.

TUMIN, MELVIN M. 'Some Disfunctions of Institutional Imbalance', *Behavioral Science*, 1 (July, 1956), pp. 218–23.

TURK, HERMAN. 'Social Cohesion Through Variant Values: Evidence from Medical Role Relations', *American Sociological Review*, 28 (February, 1963), pp. 28–37.

USHENKO, A. P. 'Problem of Causal Influence, A Refutation of Hume', *Philosophy of Science*, 9 (April, 1942), pp. 132–8.

VANCE, ROBERT B. 'Toward Social Dynamics', *American Sociological Review*, 10 (April, 1945), pp. 123–31.

WADDINGTON, C. H. 'True and False Teleology', *Nature*, 145 (May 4, 1940), p. 705.

WANDE, B. 'Origin of Causal Necessity', *Journal of Philosophy*, 56 (May 21, 1959), pp. 493–500.

WEINBERG, J. 'Idea of Causal Efficacy', *Journal of Philosophy*, 47 (July 6, 1951), pp. 397–407.

WILLIAMS, ROBIN M. 'Unity and Diversity in Modern America', *Social Forces*, 36 (October, 1957), pp. 1–8.

WISDOM, J. O. 'Criteria for Causal Determination and Functional Relationship', *Mind*, 54 (October, 1945), pp. 323–41.

Index